THE ILLUSTRATED HISTORY OF GOLF

For my mother and in memory of my father who not only inspired me to play golf,

and to love this wonderful game, but also collaborated with me

in the writing of this book before he died.

THE ILLUSTRATED HISTORY OF GOLF

MITCHELL PLATTS

PARKGATE
BOOKS

First published in 2000 by
PRC Publishing Ltd,
Kiln House, 210 New Kings Road, London SW6 4NZ

This edition published in 2000 by
Parkgate Books
London House
Great Eastern Wharf
Parkgate Road
London
SW11 4NQ

British Library Cataloguing in Publication Data:
A catalogue record for this book is available from the British Library.

ISBN 1 902616 72 3

Printed and bound in Hong Kong

ACKNOWLEDGMENTS

The publisher wishes to thank the following for kindly supplying the photography for this book:

© ALLSPORT for front cover (main image) and pages 83, 110, 111, 127, 136-137, 144, 152 (bottom), 153, 160 (bottom), 161, 163, 168, 209 and

back cover image; The Hulton Getty Picture Collection for front cover (inset top right) and pages 7, 9, 11, 12, 13, 14, 15, 16 (bottom), 19, 22

(both), 23, 25, 26, 28, 29, 30, 31, 32, 33, 34, 35, 37, 38 (both), 39, 42, 43, 51, 54, 55, 57, 58, 59, 60, 65, 66, 67, 68, 70, 79, 85 (both), 87, 88, 89, 90

(left), 96-97 (all), 98, 100-101, 102-103, 105, 117, 121, 122, 128, 129, 135 (both), 150, 160 (top), 162 and 167; © David Cannon/ALLSPORT for

front cover (inset middle right and bottom right) and pages 82, 90-91 (main), 95, 112 (bottom), 113, 119, 120, 133, 134, 139, 145, 146, 148, 149,

152 (top), 156, 169, 177, 178, 180, 182, 183, 184, 185, 186, 188, 189 (both), 197, 199, 200, 201, 204, 210, 211, 212, 213, 220, 224, 225 (bottom), 238,

248 and 254-255; © Bettmann/CORBIS for pages 4, 21, 45, 46, 49, 52, 62, 72, 73, 74-75, 76, 78, 80, 104, 106, 107, 118, 130-131, 132, 165 and 166;

© Allsport Hulton Deutsch/ALLSPORT for pages 16 (top), 36, 40, 41, 50, 56, 61, 81, 99, 109, 154 and 155; © Underwood & Underwood/CORBIS

for page 63; © Andrew Redington/ALLSPORT for pages 92-93, 114-115, 203, 216, 237 and 240; © Steve Powell/ALLSPORT for pages 112 (top),

159 and 190; © Harry How/ALLSPORT for pages 123, 231, 234, 236 and 250; © Richard Saker/ALLSPORT for page 124;

© Rick Stewart/ALLSPORT for page 125; © Gary Newkirk/ALLSPORT for pages 128 (top) and 233; © Paul Severn/ALLSPORT for pages 138,

140, 187, 202, 221, 239 and 253; © Howard Boylan/ALLSPORT for page 141; © Stephen Munday/ALLSPORT for pages 142, 147, 195 (bottom),

208, 214, 229 and 245; © Hulton-Deutsch Collection/CORBIS for page 143; © Don Morley/ALLSPORT for pages 170, 195 (top) and 207;

© Craig Jones/ALLSPORT for pages 172-173, 219, 226-227 and 241; © Chris Cole/ALLSPORT for page 175; © Trevor Jones/ALLSPORT for page

176; © Mike Powell/ALLSPORT for pages 191 and 192; © Andy Lyons/ALLSPORT for pages 193 and 225 (top); © Simon Bruty/ALLSPORT for

pages 194, 215 and 247; © Bob Martin/ALLSPORT for page 196; © Vincent Laforet/ALLSPORT for page 198; © Rusty Jarrett/ALLSPORT for page

218; © Jon Ferrey/ALLSPORT for page 223; © Brian Bahr/ALLSPORT for page 243; © Scott Barbour/ALLSPORT for page 244;

© Jamie Squire/ALLSPORT for page 246; © Nick Wilson/ALLSPORT for page 251.

CONTENTS

INTRODUCTION

The game of golf possesses a magical, almost mystical, power to entice men and women into making an unnatural movement of the body. This movement of swinging a club can cause not only physical suffering but mental anguish. Since the sole purpose of this act is to hit a little white ball around a field booby-trapped with bunkers, hedgerows, water hazards, and towering trees, with the intention of delivering it to a hole $4\frac{1}{4}$ inches in diameter, there must be many people who view golfers as foolhardy. The game can reduce a perfectly sane human being, simply wishing to escape momentarily from the hysteria of daily life behind an office desk, into a veritable nervous wreck.

But once captivated by the game of golf, no player can resist the challenge. Many a lunch has been spoiled and many a partner has been widowed because of a 19th hole examination. The happy hacker wants the world to hear about the three iron which, in the course of the other 108 shots he struck, flew unerringly to the hole with all the authority of a professional hit.

Yet there, perhaps, is the crux of the matter and the clue to the eternal fascination of golf. The alluring nature of the game is that we can, whether by accident rather than design, execute a shot of such devastating brilliance that we visualize ourselves emulating the feat in a tournament like the Open Championship at St. Andrews or the Masters Tournament at Augusta National.

Moreover, as weekend opponents, we maintain a competitive rivalry simply because golf possesses a handicap system, patterned to equalize our skills, which is the envy of all other sports. W.S. Gilbert wrote:

"All shall equal be.
The Earl, the Marquis, and the Dook,
The Groom, the Butler, and the Cook,
The Aristocrat who banks with Coutts,
The Aristocrat who cleans the boots."

Golf has the ability to make all men equal. More importantly it has the ability to remind men and women of the values of life. You can stray out of eyeshot of an opponent, but if you choose to cheat, then the only person that you really shortchange is yourself. The game was founded on integrity and that will live longer than any of us.

As Bobby Jones, whose achievements can be pitted against those of Jack Nicklaus and will, no doubt, be compared with those of Tiger Woods in time, once said: "Golf, in my view, is the most rewarding of games because it possesses a very definite value as molder or developer of character. The golfer very soon is made to realize that his most immediate, and perhaps his most potent, adversary is himself."

All I need add is that, for me, golf is the most glamorous of all sports.

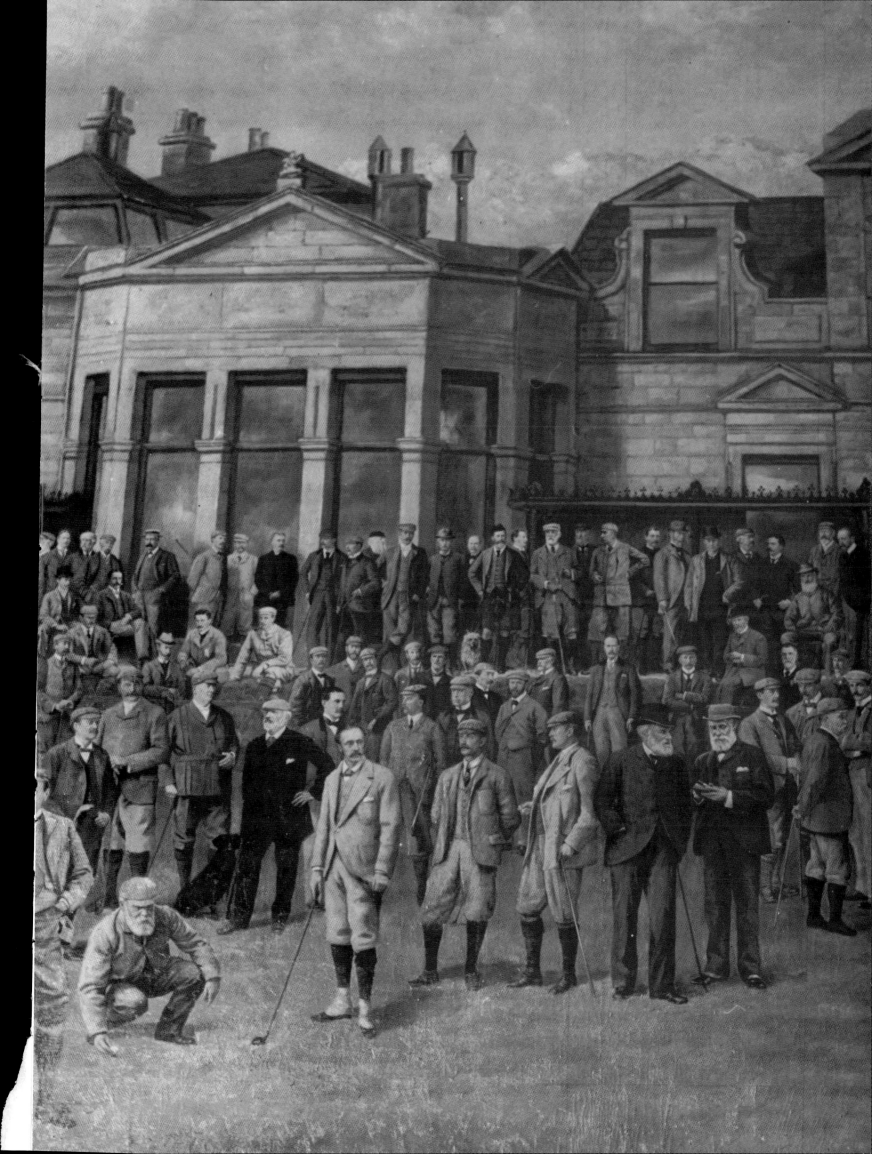

THE EVOLUTION OF THE GAME

Right: Those who start young usually excel at their chosen profession. This young golf enthusiast of the 16th century holds a golf club which differs in shape from today's version. The ball is larger than the 1.68-inch ball in use today.

The origins of golf have been traced back to the Middle Ages and the name itself is said to derive from the Dutch word for club. Certainly by the 15th century the game had gained a loyal following in Scotland, and this aroused royal displeasure.

When King James II of Scotland, more than 500 years ago, saw his archers deeply engrossed in "potting the ball" when they should have been sharpening their arrows to deal with the English invaders, he determined to put them—and the obsessive game of golf—out of bounds. He declared: "That Fute-ball and Golfe be utterly cryit doune, and nocht usit." And so a ban was entered upon the parliamentary statute books in 1457 in order to break the hold that this game had upon his fighting men.

King James must have had a pretty good crystal ball to see ahead to the time when the game with a hole in it would become an obsession and an addictive influence with future generations.

This prohibition—like most others—would have its law breakers. That, of course, would ensure the survival of the game. Today golf's participants number millions around the globe, with television reaching an armchair audience of many more millions. Yet within the confines of individual golf clubs the game has, by long-standing tradition, an honorable estate of like-minded fellows with a masonic bond which few sports can claim—and many would dearly like to emulate.

This, then, is the most honorable of games. It is one where you are expected to be as truthful and honest to yourself as you are to your opponent. How to play and score is based on trust. As a game of integrity and competitiveness played in a gentlemanly fashion it stands apart from those sports which rear temperamental followers and rivals. Of course its ups and downs bring out passionate feelings of disappointment in a player often critically directed at himself, but that in itself supercharges the challenge.

Many who view golf are both fascinated and mesmerized by the game in which a person knocks a small (1.68 inch) ball over distances of sometimes more than 500 yards in three or four blows. The same person can take the same number of strokes to hole out on a green in which a cup measuring four inches has been cut. In general if you play the game once then that is probably enough: you are hooked: dedicated whatever the cost, to achieve the goals of the game. With that comes the elation and the ecstasy.

There will always be some wrangle about the origin of golf. Who played it first? Who gave it to the world? There are a variety of contenders. Dutch old masters, for instance, show a game called kolben in a number of their paintings. Steven J.H. van Hengel, an acknowledged expert on the subject, had traced, before his untimely death, "colf" back to December 26, 1297! Then the local townsfolk of Kronenburg commemorated the relieving of their castle one year earlier by

Right: This painting, titled *Gentleman's Sport*, was executed by Lemuel Francis Abbott in about 1790 as a gift for the Society of Golfers at Blackheath. It shows an elegant gentleman playing golf accompanied by his caddy.

playing a game not dissimilar to golf with targets, such as a kitchen door, rather than a hole. The French, Italians, and Spaniards have rival claims. Stick and ball games abound, such as the Irish-Scottish pastime of shinty.

In fact almost anywhere in Europe you will find a historian claiming that golf originated in his or her country. There are documented details of the game in the Netherlands before the direct references attributed to Scotland in 1457.

Then there is a 15th century stained-glass window in England, in Gloucester Cathedral, depicting a man swinging a club-stick implement. In some sense it is true to say that all of these stick and ball games contributed to spawning the Scots game.

We know for sure that the emergence of golf, as played today, was taking place over fields and scrub in Scotland when King James II put the ban on the statute book in 1457. So while there are various rival claims about the origins of golf, the Scots can rightly claim to have developed the game.

When James IV in 1502 sent off to his "pro shop" for a set of "tools"—a set of clubs and balls from his bowmaker in Perth—the Church soon showed interest in the game too. The then Archbishop of St. Andrews allowed players to tee off on the links although never on a Sunday which might interfere with the sermon! Failure to adhere to these regulations would meet with penalties, as John Henrie and Pat Rogie discovered to their cost in 1593. They were jailed for "playing of the gowff on the links of Leith every Sabbath the time of the sermonses."

By the middle of the 18th century golf was gaining in popularity. King James VI of Scotland had ascended the throne as King James I of England and in 1744 William St. Clair, a hereditary

Grand Master mason of Scotland, formed a golf club, the Gentleman Golfers of Leith, later called the Honourable Company of Edinburgh Golfers. This club would eventually move to Musselburgh and then to Muirfield. The Leith trophy was to be the first golfing trophy and would take the form of a silver club.

More importantly these "Gentlemen of Leith" tabled the 13 rules of the Golf Manual which form the basis of those in operation today. Members were mainly masons who provided loyal support during the club's early years.

In the United States too they laid the basic foundations of the game. There, a Mr. David Deas of Charleston, South Carolina, who had emigrated to America from Scotland, purchased Scottish clubs and balls in 1743 and began setting up a golf club. There is, however, no evidence that a club was established. Even so golf owes much to gentlemen such as David Deas.

The implements (clubs) all had wooden shafts and heads, made almost solely in Scotland, and it was not until 1920 that metal shafts were produced. The canny Scots were soon exporting their golfing "tools." There are records of shipments to the United States around 1750, following that first consignment to Charleston, which suggests that golf was in the swing in other parts of America too.

Unlike today, when players have matched sets with a system of numbering, the game then had its own traditional lore, with such clubs as the cleek (two or three iron), brassie, spoon, baffle, mashie (five iron), and niblick (eight or nine iron). Clubs like the wedge and putter were to follow later.

During these early days golf courses were often rough-and-ready affairs. The game could evolve around a piece of parkland or any piece of

ground, provided one could pitch a ball and provided there was, say, a rabbit burrow to act as a
hole. One of the first laid-out courses was that at
Leith where the gentlemen would play with
friends who shared their desire to find fresh
"greens" to conquer.

Some would take the boat north from their
new home at Musselburgh to a spot called St.
Andrews. Within a short space of time a club
would be formed there. These "links" close to the
sea proved very popular, the short, weedy grass
allowing the ball to run freely and smoothly. It

Right: William St. Clair of Roslin, painted here by Sir George Chalmers, caused the Old Course at St. Andrews to be reduced to 18 holes because of his astonishing scoring exploits. He favored, as most of his contemporaries did, an exaggerated closed stance in order to give the feathery ball a firm strike.

Left: Henry Callender in the
uniform of the Blackheath Club,
engraved by Ward (1812) following a
painting by Lemuel Abbott.

Above: A humorous sketch published in 1863 shows golfers enjoying an afternoon at Blackheath Golf Club.

was, of course, also easier to make contact with the ball in play. And there was the added advantage that there was less wear and tear on the clubs and the featheries—not inexpensive items.

These early balls or featheries, as they were called, were made of a stitched leather pouch which was stuffed with goose or other bird feathers, impounded very tightly into a small, sewn ball and waterproofed with a white lead-type paint. They were expensive to produce and subject to deterioration, so players couldn't afford to lose many of them. At first the implements were made of hazel or ash with heads of blackthorn-beech or applewood. They were strong enough to withstand the rugged ground on which they would be swung. Later craftsmen developed these with varied angled heads into a combination of six woods and two irons to a set. As the number of

clubs carried in the bag increased woods lost ground in popularity to irons.

How players dressed varied. Players who were not members of a club would play in their everyday clothing, wearing hats and coats that went right down to their hob-nailed boots. The more elite clubbers wore a sort of uniform and would be accompanied by their lads (caddies), who would carry under their arms the clubs of their master.

From these beginnings materialized the format of today's clubs. And when King William IV became patron of the Society of St. Andrews he honored them with the title of the R. and A.—the Royal and Ancient Golf Club of St. Andrews. In fact the Honourable Company at Edinburgh had appeared on the scene first. But it was the R. and A. that took charge.

Westward HO   April 1872

Above: This sketch from 1872 shows golfers in action at the Westward Ho! links in Devon.

The club had been founded in 1754 when "22 Noblemen and Gentlemen, being admirers of the ancient and healthful exercise of the Golf" subscribed for a silver club to be played for annually. Even the silver club idea had been "stolen" from the Honourable Company, as in 1744 the Edinburgh Town Council had presented the Company with a silver club as a prize for outstanding members.

The Honourable Company, now based at Muirfield on the Firth of Forth to the east of Edinburgh, could boast a first when John Rattray won a club competition played over Leith's five-hole layout. Rattray became their first captain. It was St. Andrews, however, that was to became the home of golf. Not surprisingly the Scots regard the city with enormous pride. It was at St. Andrews, for instance, that William St. Clair played a round in 1764 of 121 strokes and, because of his contemptuous treatment of the links, it was decided there and then to reduce the number of holes from 22 to 18.

The Royal and Ancient became the ruling body when in 1834 King William IV conferred the title upon them. Before this the early "hackers" would play over common, links, or scrubland on rudimentary courses consisting of a varied number of holes. The length between holes did not often vary a great deal in terms of individual distance. The shorter hole courses, however, would require a number of circuits. At some of these there would be up to 25 holes. Contests here were of match-play, with wagers struck on the outcome in head-to-head challenges and bets struck on the results at each hole. Matches were sometimes organized by subscription: the

Right: An 1865 photograph of players at the Royal and Ancient, St. Andrews. As with today's golfers, these gentleman would refresh themselves and talk over the game at the very popular 19th hole.

Below Right: British golfers Captain Hay Wemyss (right), "Old" Tom Morris (left), and Allan Robertson with his clubs under his arm (center), at St. Andrews in Scotland. "Old Tom" Morris won the 1862 Open Championship by a record 13 strokes. "Old Tom" and his son "Young Tom" became the only father and son to hold successive Open titles when "Old Tom" became the oldest player to win a title, aged 46 years and 99 days, in 1867, and "Young Tom" won in 1868. In the following year he won again and his father finished second.

competitor would agree to attend the ground and either pay dues to the club's "messenger" or a sum of about a shilling which would cover the cost of food and drink too.

The match would start in those days with the ball teed up on a mound of earth or sand. The game would attract a gallery of ladies and gentlemen out for a stroll. Afterward the competitors would adjourn to the "19th" to partake of refreshments. Baillie Glass's and the Black Bull Tavern were popular haunts in St. Andrews.

And by all accounts there was ample consumption of alcoholic beverages, with some indi-

viduals downing several bottles at a sitting. When one considers that wagers were frequently struck in stakes of liquid assets it is no small wonder that they enjoyed their after-match activities.

Following St. Andrews, clubs were formed more readily. Among these were Aberdeen and Crail on Scotland's east coast, and then others such as North Berwick. In 1851, Prestwick, which was to be the home of the first 12 Open Championships, was established. St. Andrews, however, continued to take the lead and it was there in 1858 that the R. and A. framed a competition for a match over 18 holes. Allan Robertson, the accepted champion of the time, won, but with his death in 1859 there arose a question. Who would be the new champion? And where?

Willie Park and Prestwick, a small fishing village on the west coast of Scotland, would provide the answers. They would also transform the game. For the eight who turned up at Prestwick's 12-hole course not only vied to be Robertson's successor but also introduced stroke-play as a form of competition. More importantly, in 1860 the Open Championship had been born— although not without a good deal of rancor.

The problem was that Major J.O. Fairlie, the Prestwick member who had proposed the competition, had invited professionals only. Many leading amateurs argued that it was unfair that they had been excluded and that it was not a true championship without their presence. In fact the competition had been arranged to determine Scotland's finest golfer. Major Fairlie was compelled to announce that the:

"Belt to be played for tomorrow and on all other occasions until it be otherwise resolved shall be open to all the world!"

It remains so to this day.

So the "half" Open was won on October 17 by Willie Park of the Musselburgh Club. He shot 174 for the 36 holes played—three rounds on the 12-hole course—with "Old Tom" Morris finishing second. The prize was a red Moroccan leather belt with silver mountings, which was presented to Willie Park by the Earl of Eglinton.

By then the feathery had been overtaken by the new gutta-percha ball. This was a Malayan rubberized compound that served to give longer life and smoothness, although following its birth in 1848 it was to give way in 1870 to its offspring,

the gutsy, which incorporated cork and leather into the rubberized compound. Some credit the invention of this new ball to a Dr. Paterson of St. Andrews. He had taken the rubber sole of his old shoe and had melted it to ply around the gutta-percha. However, its performance did not always match that of the old feathery. Experience promotes invention; as the smooth ball suffered knocks and chips as it was struck, so it was discovered, unintentionally, that pits and dimples would improve the performance of the ball. Indeed as the ball became more durable a hammer came to be used to indent its outer shell so as to obtain a better flight.

Britain's adventurous young men were now beginning to take their golf game with them to far-flung parts of the world and forming their own golf clubs in these new regions. Exactly when golf was first played in the United States has never been clearly established, although there are a number of references to the game that date back to the beginning of the 19th century.

At Savannah there hangs an invitation dated 1811 to a golf club ball for a Miss Eliza Johnston. There is little doubt that there was a club in existence but there are no records to support the theory that golf was in fact played there. It was, however, played in Yonkers, New York, by John Reid and some friends in 1888. He had asked a friend who was taking a trip to Scotland to call in to the shop of "Old Tom" Morris at St. Andrews and purchase some equipment. Mr. Reid, born in Dunfermline in 1840, had learned to play the game at Musselburgh. Now he developed a course, initially of three holes, which was to be called the St. Andrew's Club of Yonkers on Hudson. At a similar time, maybe even a couple of years earlier, another club, Oakhurst, had been formed in West Virginia by Scottish settlers. However, Reid, rightly or wrongly, is credited as being the "Father of American Golf."

Yonkers on Hudson later moved its course to an old apple orchard where members played over six holes and eager pioneers were to become known as The Apple Tree Gang. Club members there were also known for their habit of partaking of refreshments from picnic baskets at the final hole. At the Merion Golf Club today, instead of a pennant at the top of the flagstick, there is a small wicker basket that recalls the custom of those pioneering days of golf in the United States.

Early published versions of the qualifications needed to play the game, which was, after all, a popular Scottish pastime, must surely have deterred many a would-be player. One early account gives the following detailed description:

"The game requires much brawn and vigour. Accompanied by a servant (caddie) it requires men of exceptional physique, necessary to run to the full. His servant, carrying the required tools, follows and also clears the way ahead. Strong lungs, firm muscles of the legs and endless stamina are essential.

"On an expanse of land holes are dug a foot or so deep and four inches in diameter. The holes should circumference the field at distances of up to 500 yards. The implements of the game comprise around ten types with a round ball of gutta-percha which should be painted white and weigh about two ounces so that it can enter the hole and be easily removed. The implements (clubs) are of various angled head shapes to lift the ball

to where the holes are and to sink it into the hole itself. The reason for the variation of the angles of the tools is to suit the situation and distances the player finds himself in when he bats the ball.

"The player starts from the first starting point and with accuracy aims towards the desired hole be it 100 or 500 yards away. Once the ball is in the air he runs forward caddie following (with the rest of the tools)—and by luck or judgement aims to put the ball into the hole. Then he is off to the next hole, before his opponent. All the time his caddie attends his master, ready to hand the desired implement required for the next play. The said servant should be an expert in his selection of the tool for which ever the master's next play requires.

"The player who is first to the hole holds preference whilst his opponent must wait until he has spooned the ball from the hole. The opponent then plays his turn whilst the first player plays off towards the next hole. This follows around the field and should the ball be put past the hole it must be knocked back until entering the hole. Should the other player distance his ball nearer the hole this gains him the ground."

These observations may well have been a deterrent to a would-be aspiring American hoping to take up the game of golf. But in fact the United States would bring its own ingenuity of equipment and adjustments to the game of golf.

During these early days, when the game was really starting to take off, a spate of enterprising individuals cashed in on the game's sudden popularity in America (by 1900 there were more courses there than in Britain). Mr. Tom Bendelow marked out a playing course within a day for a $25 charge. The course offered little more than a

Left: A photograph of "Old Tom" Morris who, at the age of 40, won his first Open Championship in 1861, then returned to Prestwick 12 months later to successfully defend his title with a margin of 13 strokes—a record that still stands. He won again in 1864 and for a fourth time in 1867, by which time he had returned to St. Andrews to become greenkeeper at the Royal and Ancient. "Old Tom" held that position until 1903 and played in the Open until 1906. He died in 1908.

flat or circular piece of rough, patchy grass, but such was the increasing interest in the game that he, or his paymasters, had no difficulty in selling his services.

Charles Blair Macdonald was another colorful character. His knowledge of the game came from his years as a student at the St. Andrews University. Big, bluff, and self-opinionated, he was for all this a very good player—but not a good loser. After failing to win an invitation tournament which had been organized by the Newport Golf Club on Rhode Island in 1894, he ranted about how absurd it was to have a stroke-play in an amateur championship.

One month later he was to lose again, albeit in the final, when the St. Andrew's club agreed to play a match-play tournament. Old Mac, who on the final day drank a bottle of champagne as an antidote for a hangover, could still find excuses for his defeat. The result never made it into the record books. No doubt, however, some of this ranting and raving by a poor loser prompted some of the prominent golfing administrators of the leading clubs, of which Macdonald was one, to form in December 1894, the United States Golf Association. And who should become its very first amateur champion in 1895—none other than one Charles Blair Macdonald. He was now to throw the full force of his influential and powerful personality behind the authoritative body.

The ten years leading up to the 20th century saw American golf boom as 1,000 courses were built. The best of these were credited to Macdonald's skills of planning, his Chicago course being a particularly fine example. High standards followed and many clubs flourished under the patronage of the wealthy. Most also had a Scottish professional who taught and supervised.

The first U.S. Open at Newport, Rhode Island which took place in 1895, was won by an Englishman, Horace Rawlins. He had come over to work at the Newport Club and his scores of 91 and 82 were sufficient to beat off his opponents. His prize was $150. The following year he achieved second place to Jimmy Foulis, who was a Scot, at Shinnecock Hills, Long Island, New York.

One of the most important and significant items in golfing history was introduced around that time by an American. Coburn Haskell, an employee of the Goodrich Tire and Rubber Company, was responsible for the arrival of the rubber-cored ball. This new ball had its critics but its introduction was essentially a watershed for golf. Elastic thread was wound, under extreme tension, around a rubber core which was then encased in a layer of gutta-percha.

Confirmation of its excellence came at Royal Liverpool, otherwise known as Hoylake, in 1902—one year after its arrival—when Sandy Herd won the Open Championship. His achievement came after playing the same ball for all 72 holes—the Haskell ball! It was the end of the gutty and the start of a new era of startling golfing endeavor.

The Haskell ball was now appearing in British shops at a cost of two shillings. But it was soon to become the subject of controversy and scrutiny. The R. and A. and the U.S.G.A., the dual arbiters of the game, were together in agreement in 1920 that the ball should weigh no more than 1.62 ounces and should have a diameter of not less than 1.62 inches.

It was a different story 11 years later when the "big ball" with a maximum weight of 1.55 ounces and a minimum size of 1.68 inches was introduced in the United States. Twelve months

Distributors for all makes of Golf Balls, full line in stock.

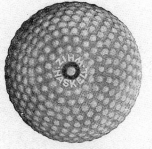

RUBBER CORE GOLF BALLS

Per doz.

Haskell Whiz	$6.00
Haskell Streak	6.00
Black White Flyer	6.00
White Cover Liquid Centre	6.00
Hand Made	7.50
White Bramble, flat marking	9.00
Black Diamond	6.00
Red, White and Blue Spaulding Balls	9.00
Spaulding Blue and Red Dots	6.00
Dimple Glory	9.00

LINEOGRAPH.
Strongly recommended for marking out Tennis Courts, Base Ball, Polo and Foot Ball grounds, each ...... $12.00 to $35.00

Large stock of seasoned shafts in the rough or finished. Timber all seasoned naturally and not kiln dried.

later the weight limit was increased to 1.62 ounces. The difference between 1.62 and 1.68 inches may not seem great, but Americans soon discovered that the bigger ball was easier to hit. It sat up more invitingly on the fairways and most found it easier to both chip and putt with. It took experimenting with the ball in the 1960s by the Professional Golfers' Association in Britain before the Royal and Ancient made the big ball compulsory in the Open Championship from 1974. Today the small ball is part of the past.

Clubs, too, had changed from the old hickory and persimmon types to laminates, composition and, in the latter part of the 20th century, the metal headed driver became universally popular. Because of the short supply of hickory the switch was made to steel shafts. The U.S.G.A. cleared these for play in 1926 and the R. and A. followed four years later. In 1929, rustless chrome would extend the longevity of shafts.

Far Right: An early photograph, from 1911, shows a Ms. Kyle driving off at Portrush in County Antrim, Northern Ireland, wearing skirts that might have suited the etiquette of the time but did nothing for a golfer's swing!

Right: A 1938 photograph of Mr. Jamie Anderson inspecting golf clubs at St. Andrews. Innovations in club design revolutionized the game as much as the adoption of the rubber core ball.

The slight differences between the R. and A. and the U.S.G.A. were all but erased when in 1950 the two governing bodies came together with a uniform set of rules for the game throughout the world. The R. and A. had laid down the original rules of golf back in the 18th century and in 1897 they had appointed a Rules of Golf Committee. America's U.S.G.A. had also framed their own rules. Today, the two august bodies renew the ruling from time to time and they provide joint decisions when asked to resolve important questions wherever golf is played.

The first club for women golfers was the North Devon Ladies Club of Westward Ho!, England, founded in 1868. At first women were restricted to the use of putters only—adopting the physical style of swing as practiced by the men was frowned upon! That didn't stop the determined golfers, however, and the sport began to blossom for them when in 1872 the London Scottish Ladies Club was formed. One of their members, a Mrs. Pearson, formed a Ladies' Golf Union in 1893. There was no stopping the growth of the game. A British Women's Amateur Championship was played, albeit over nine holes, at Royal Lytham and St. Annes, Lancashire, in 1893 and won by Lady Scott. She won it again for the next two years under match-play rules.

American women were quick to follow with their first official event being staged in 1895. Beatrice Heyt, at the age of 16, won the U.S. Ladies' title in 1896. Like Lady Scott she won three times in succession and the women's game, like the men's, flourished. Competition between Great Britain and the United States was given a boost when Margaret and Harriot Curtis presented the Curtis Cup. In 1932, this cup was awarded for the first time to the United States following the team's victory at Wentworth, Surrey.

The Curtis Cup is contested every other year like the men's counterparts—the Walker Cup, born in 1922, and the Ryder Cup, first played in 1927. Not until 1952 were British women to notch a victory although there was a more famous result in 1958, when for the first time they managed a half with the Americans on their own soil. That came after the era of Miss Joyce Wethered, later Lady Heathcoat Amory, whose classic swing, still regarded today as near perfection, was to earn for her a succession of one title after another.

In Glenna Collett the United States, too, produced an exceptionally talented player as she recorded six championship wins from 1922 to 1935. But America's first winner of the British Ladies' title did not come until 1947 when Miss Mildred Didrikson, better known as Mrs. Babe Zaharias, took the title. She was followed the next year by Louise Suggs.

On both sides of the Atlantic, as the years rolled on, the great names of this glorious game etched their deeds into the history books. Names like Harry Vardon and Cecil Leitch, Bobby Jones and Joyce Wethered, Henry Cotton and Patty Berg, Ben Hogan and Babe Zaharias, Arnold Palmer and Mickey Wright, Jack Nicklaus and Kathy Whitworth, Tom Watson and Nancy Lopez, Nick Faldo and Laura Davies, Tiger Woods and Annika Sorenstam.

The men, assisted by others from around the globe like Peter Thomson and Greg Norman of Australia, Gary Player and Ernie Els of South Africa, and Severiano Ballesteros and Jose Maria Olazábal of Spain, had lit the blue touchpaper. The women, too, craved to be part of the game as it exploded in popularity. Millions flocked to the fairways, magnetized by a game that was based on integrity, fired by invention, and played by inspired individuals.

GOLF TEES OFF

Right: British golfers "Old Tom" Morris and Charlie Hunter at the first Open Championship at Prestwick, Ayrshire, in 1860. Tom lost on this occasion to Willie Park of Musselburgh.

In 1860, the first Open Championship was played at Prestwick, a small fishing village on the west coast of Scotland. Organized by club secretary Major Jock Fairlie it was a competition between eight players to find a new champion following the death the previous year of Allan Robertson, considered at the time to be unbeatable.

Held over three rounds on a 12-hole course which measured some 3,799 yards, the championship was won by Willie Park of Musselburgh with a total of 174. Only one English club, Blackheath, acknowledged to be the oldest club "south of the border" was represented.

What Park's two-stroke win from "Old Tom" Morris did was to publicize the game to such an extent that three major English clubs were founded. These were Westward Ho!—or the Royal North Devon Golf Club as it is known today—the Liverpool Golf Club, later to be honored with the Royal prefix and known to many as Hoylake, and the London Scottish Club at Wimbledon.

Yet the 1860 event was not truly an Open. For no amateurs had been invited to take part although, following representation, this was rectified the following year in order to ensure its authenticity as an open tournament. Park had put together rounds of 55, 59, and 60 in 1860. He was to score 54-54-59, seven shots better, 12 months later but he was still beaten by four shots as "Old Tom" Morris handed in cards of 54, 56, and 53 for a total of 163.

Prestwick was celebrated as a course, its 12 holes spread over lofty sandhills. For the most part the holes were out of sight, so the golfer would experience a fascinating excitement as he lofted over the mountains of sand and clambered uphill to see how near the hole his ball had rolled. Or for that matter, how far away it was!

"Old Tom" Morris, however, was a master at Prestwick. He also won in 1862 and he recaptured the title in 1864 after Park had regained it. Born in St. Andrews on June 16, 1821, Morris became apprenticed to Allan Robertson in the ball-making trade. He had, in 1851, been taken to Prestwick by Major Fairlie, so he knew the course well, although in 1865, when Andrew Strath won, and when official scoring cards were issued for the first time, Morris returned to St. Andrews where he was to hold the position as greenkeeper to the Royal and Ancient until 1904. Willie Park won for a third time in 1866 but then back, once again, came Morris to take the title in 1867 for a fourth occasion. "Old Tom" Morris had had his last win—but the red leather Championship belt would stay in the family for all time.

For in 1868 "Young Tom" Morris, "Old Tom's" son, scored a Championship best—149—for the first of three successive wins. In 1868 he set something of a record by scoring the first hole-in-one in the Championship. Yet he was to create a far bigger stir by winning the title again in 1869 and 1870. Under the rules the belt, presented by

the late Earl of Eglinton, became his property after his third win, and so in 1871 no Championship was held. This sparked an appeal, which led to the members at Musselburgh, Prestwick, and St. Andrews, raising funds for purchasing a cup for annual competition. The Open Championship was back to stay, although, unlike the belt, it was deemed that the cup could never become the absolute property of one winner. The new trophy was a silver claret jug. It still is today and the winner receives a replica. The staging of the Open was to be shared by those three clubs which had subscribed to the trophy, which led to the introduction of the rota system.

With the move to St. Andrews in 1873 the competition changed. There were now two rounds of 18 holes each, and Tom Kidd won that year with scores of 91 and 88. "Young Tom" Morris was joint third and he was runner-up the following year to Mungo Park at Musselburgh. Sadly his days were numbered for in 1875 he died on Christmas Day at the age of 24—he had never fully recovered from the shock of his young wife's untimely death.

At the Open at St. Andrews in 1876 trouble loomed. David Strath had tied with Bob Martin but there was a protest against Strath for playing his second shot to the 17th when there were still players on the green. Strath, annoyed at the objection and the committee's long-winded post-mortem, stormed out and refused to take part in a play-off, with the result that Martin was declared the winner.

Jamie Anderson, born at St. Andrews and regarded as the very embodiment of machine-like accuracy, won the title for the next three years and Bob Ferguson, a former caddie from Musselburgh, emulated him in 1880, 1881, and

1882. Thus Scottish golfers retained their grip on the Open Championship until in 1890 Mr. John Ball Junior, whose father owned the Royal Hotel at Hoylake, became the first amateur to win the title. His credentials as a golfer of considerable ability were reaffirmed when, between 1888 and 1912, he won the Amateur Championship on no fewer than eight occasions.

The first Amateur Championship had taken place in 1885 at Royal Liverpool. It was not the success it should have been—invitations were sent only to certain clubs and an administrative faux pas resulted in there being three semi-finalists! Thus A.F. MacFie received a bye at that stage and it was not until the Royal and Ancient took control of the event in 1920 that it was decided to recognize MacFie's win. This recognition also meant that the 1885 competition became regarded as the first. Bernard Darwin, authoritative writer, England international from 1902 to 1924, and captain of the R. and A. in 1934–35, captured it perfectly—MacFie became retrospectively canonized!

Following two successes by Horace G. Hutchinson who was to become the first Englishman to captain the R. and A., Ball won his first Amateur Championship in 1888. By winning both the Open Championship and the Amateur Championship he shares with Bobby Jones, who was to do so in 1930, the distinction of taking both titles in the same year.

Hugh Kirkaldy won the day again for the professionals in 1891. But in 1892, ironically when the prize fund soared from less than £30 to £110 and an entry fee was imposed, Harold Horsfall Hilton won. For the first time the Open was played over 72 holes and it was staged by the Honourable Company, not at Musselburgh but at

Right: Harold Hilton won the Open Championship in 1892, the year in which the Championship was extended to 72 holes, and again in 1897. In 1911 he became the first man and the only Briton to complete the double of the British and United States Amateur Championships.

their new home at Muirfield. Some observers expressed the belief that the 18 holes at Muirfield had a sameness about them that meant they were not such a reliable test of golfing ability as the nine holes at Musselburgh.

Hilton was to win the Open again, at Royal Liverpool in 1897, and in 1911 he became the only British player to hold both the Amateur Championship and the American equivalent at the same time.

Golf, and in particular British golf, was now to enjoy a golden age. The game would be domi-

nated by three individuals known collectively as The Great Triumvirate—John Henry Taylor, a West Countryman, Harry Vardon, a Channel Islander, and James Braid, a Scot. They dominated the Open Championship by chalking up a total of 16 wins between them in 21 years, and ruled the golfing scene until the First World War. In 1894, the Championship crossed south of the border for the first time to St. George's, Sandwich, and there, appropriately, J.H. Taylor became the first English professional to win. He won again in 1895, 1900, 1909, and 1913. Harry Vardon, the

Open champion record holder achieved six wins in 1896, 1898, 1899, 1903, 1911, and 1914, and James Braid triumphed with a succession of wins in 1901, 1905, 1906, 1908, and 1910.

The game had never known such giants; even "Old Tom" and "Young Tom" had held the winner's belt only four times each. Vardon, the champion of champions, was born in Grouville, Jersey, in 1870. He set patterns and style of play that are practiced and copied today. His famous "Vardon grip"—the little finger of the right hand overlaps the forefinger of the left—was not invented by him but he did popularize it. Today it is the accepted grip of most golfers, even if Jack Nicklaus employs an interlocking grip—entwining the two fingers—and some, although this is rare, favor a double-handed "baseball" grip. Vardon, like Taylor, was of average build and in keeping with this he liked to have a soft feel with the club. In essence, he introduced the modern upright swing; bringing style, sweetness, and accuracy to the game.

Vardon's great consistency started tales of how he could make carbon-copy shots over two

Above: The Great Triumvirate of (from left to right) J.H. Taylor, James Braid, and Harry Vardon, pose with Sandy Herd (right). Taylor, Braid, and Vardon dominated the Open Championship from 1894 until 1914, although Herd managed to record a victory at Hoylake in 1902.

Above: Harry Vardon introduced the modern upright swing to golf and was noted for his consistency. Here he is seen chipping during a challenge match.

separate rounds, playing out the same divots as those of his previous rounds.

The Vardon way certainly changed the way that golf was to be played for evermore.

Vardon had come to England from the island of Jersey in the Channel Islands so that he could gain more experience. He had been first a pageboy then a manservant and next an undergardener. Now he was keen to follow in the footsteps of his brother Tom who was making a living

from the game. He took a job at Bury Golf Club, although he eventually moved on to Ganton. In 1893, at the age of 23, he entered his first Open. He finished one stroke ahead of his brother but 22 shots behind Willie Auchterlonie, who won with a set of seven clubs that he had made himself. Shortly afterward, Auchterlonie was to found a famous club-making business in St. Andrews where he had been born.

Golf, with its roots firmly in Scotland, had for

the most part been played on the linksland— sandy coastal strips of what was virtually waste ground, formed after the last Ice Age when the seas withdrew, and where the raw, biting winds encouraged players to adopt a wide stance and hit the ball low. Vardon, however, adopted a different approach. He had a narrow stance and an upright swing. He would hit the ball high, imparting the kind of backspin on the ball that was foreign in his day and that led to the kind of precision which had seemed to be only a dream until that time.

Vardon, then, was to become very much a cult figure and one whose achievements would stand the test of time. Vardon, Taylor, and Braid had all been born within 13 months of each other and it was Taylor who struck first in the Open Championship with his win in 1894. He retained the Championship 12 months later when at St. Andrews he put together a last round of 78—

Right: J.H. Taylor photographed
looking very workmanlike in 1908.
Taylor was the first of the Great
Triumvirate to win an Open
Championship when he was
victorious in 1894.

four shots better than anyone else had achieved
that day—to win by four from Sandy Herd who
had an 85.

Taylor, who lived until he was 92 and retired
from golf only six years before that, did much to
promote golf as a profession as well as to help
found the Professional Golfers' Association.
Indeed he did so much to raise the status of the

professional golfer that Bernard Darwin wrote,
"He turned a feckless company into a self-
respecting and respected body of men."

Born at Northam in North Devon on March
19, 1871, Taylor had little education. He left
school at 11 and he spent most of his formative
days around the golf course at Westward Ho! in
his native county. Unlike James Braid, Taylor was a

small man with a quick temper. His craftsmanship as a clubmaker also earned him a high reputation, but it is on his shot-making that he should be judged. A fine iron player, he was smart around the greens and deadly on them—as many of his defeated opponents found to their cost.

The start of his run of Open Championship wins was itself a part of history as he became the first English professional to take possession of the silver claret jug. The two other English winners prior to Taylor—Hilton and Ball—were both amateurs. His victory at St. George's gave him great satisfaction, but not as much as that at St. Andrews in 1895 as he had vowed that he would win on Scottish soil. The historic and notable sequence of victories that The Great Triumvirate were to achieve had begun.

The first of Taylor and Vardon's great head-to-head duels was to unfold at Muirfield in 1896. It was an exciting week, with the Honourable Company of Edinburgh Golfers receiving much praise for the changes they had made to the course since Hilton's win in 1892. (On one day the wind had been so light that it was insufficient

Above: A scene during the Amateur Championship at Westward Ho!, Royal North Devon, in June 1912, where John Ball beat Abe Mitchell at the 38th in the final.

Right: Champion golfer John Ball, the first amateur to win the Open Championship title. Between 1888 and 1912 he won the Amateur Championship on no fewer than eight occasions.

to drive the windmill which supplied the club-house with water!)

Taylor led by three entering the final round but he shot 80 to Vardon's 77 and so the two great players went into a 36-hole play-off, which Vardon won by four shots. Hilton returned to win in 1897 at Royal Liverpool but Vardon regained the trophy in 1898 when new regulations were enforced. It had been decided to implement what today is called the "cut." Any player 20 strokes or more behind the halfway leader was excluded from the final two rounds, although there was the proviso that a minimum of 32 players should qualify for the latter stages. Vardon won by one shot from Willie Park Junior

who had been champion in 1887 and 1889. In 1899 he won again, this time at St. George's which boosted a record entry of 101 (albeit that many withdrew). Vardon cruised home by five shots ahead of Jack White who was to have his day in 1904. It was Taylor's turn again at St. Andrews in 1900. Vardon, who was runner-up, had been on tour to the United States where demand for his exhibitions kept him very busy. He did, however, find the time to go to Chicago that year for the U.S. Open which he won.

Braid had finished third behind Taylor and Vardon in 1900. Twelve months later he finished first, with Vardon second, and Taylor third, so establishing The Great Triumvirate. Born at Elie,

Above: J.H. Taylor joins other golfing champions in instructing customers at Harrods store, London, in the correct method of addressing the ball. Taylor won the Open Championship five times between 1894 and 1913.

Right: James Braid, who was a
member of the Great Triumvirate,
won the Open Championship in
1901, 1905, 1906, 1908, and 1910.

Fife, on February 6, 1870, Braid was a joiner by trade, but he went to London in 1893 to work as a clubmaker and he turned professional three years later.

It took Braid very little time to establish himself. He took part in a challenge match with Taylor in which they finished level. Next he teamed up with Sandy Herd in a £400 challenge match over four courses which was won by Taylor and Vardon. Even so Braid had by now proved himself a player of consistent merit.

Braid's record deserves examining. He was to win the Open on five occasions. He was runner-up four times, third twice, and on no fewer than 15 occasions he finished among the top five. He also won the P.G.A. match-play title five times, which reflects the strength of his game.

In fact Braid's temperament was perfect for such a frustrating game. His imperturbability was as important a quality as his powerful play. Even when there was every chance of driving into trouble he remained calm and composed on the fairways and it was said that "nobody could be as wise as James Braid looked." A modest man, he was one of the founder members of the Professional Golfers' Association.

Vardon came back to win in 1903, edging his brother Tom into second place at Prestwick, and that in itself was a minor miracle. His health had declined when in 1901 he had contracted tuberculosis. This had imposed some restrictions on his playing and was certainly instrumental in keeping him from winning more tournaments than he actually did for he was not to achieve his record total until much later.

For the moment it was Braid who dominated the scene. He won again in 1905 and 1906 and, after Arnaud Massy of France had at Royal Liverpool in 1907 become the first overseas winner of the Open Championship, he stormed home by no fewer than eight shots at Prestwick in 1908. Taylor bounced back in 1909 when for the first time the Open was staged at Royal Cinque Ports, Deal, but Braid was not to be deterred by this.

Left: James Braid plays from a bunker at the second hole at Royal St George's, Sandwich, during the Open Championship in 1928 which was won by Walter Hagen.

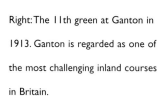

Right: There are bunkers and bunkers, but the "crater" at the 10th at Berwick-upon-Tweed, presented a monumental challenge to those foolish or unfortunate enough to visit it.

Right: The 11th green at Ganton in 1913. Ganton is regarded as one of the most challenging inland courses in Britain.

At St. Andrews in 1910 Braid won for the fifth time in ten years. It was a remarkable achievement by this six foot three inch accomplished stylist who retained his game almost until his death at the age of 80. On his 78th birthday he shot a 74. He continued playing competitively through to his sixties, never losing his touch. Braid was immensely popular—he was a jovial man with an astute knowledge of and a passionate love for the game. He didn't mince his words, but he was still regarded as a lively conversationalist. People were drawn to him as a partner not only because he was a great golfer, but because he was a person of intelligence and character.

In 1911 Vardon again ascended the winner's podium at Royal St. George's. He led comfortably at one stage, but then he faltered and only just managed to tie with Massy, the Frenchman. Vardon, however, showed his dogged determination by overcoming Massy in the play-off. A popular win, yes, but a popular venue, no.

The Open Championship, and the game of golf, were becoming increasingly popular, so much so that the accommodation in Sandwich had largely been snapped up by traders keen to do business there. This rather upset the players, as many had to stay at Deal, which meant in those days a tricky journey morning and night on irreg-

ular trains, and it was implied by some observers that the state of affairs had led to much grumbling among the professionals.

Vardon, of course, went home to his club at South Hems, near London, supremely happy until beaten into second place the following year by Edward Ray at Muirfield.

Ray had also been born on the small island of Jersey, though seven years later than Vardon, and his trademark was that he often played with a pipe clenched between his teeth. He could drive the ball a great distance and he also possessed great powers of recovery.

By 1913 Taylor was back, winning this time at Royal Liverpool. It was a fact that until then not one of The Great Triumvirate had won at Hoylake, although Taylor was to come home eight shots ahead of Ray, the defending champion.

Rejected by the army during the First World War because of physical disabilities with his feet and eyes—the latter at times affected his judgment of play—Taylor might have established himself as the all-time record holder of the Open Championship. But along came Harry Vardon.

The First World War was imminent and Taylor and Vardon, now with five wins apiece, had

Above: James Braid plays out of a bunker. A superb golfer and a man of great character he was extremely popular with spectators and other golfers alike.

Right: Ted Ray (left) and Harry
Vardon photographed on
October 4, 1912, after Vardon had
won the £400 professional golf
tournament final at Sunningdale.

only one more chance before the Championship went into abeyance until 1920. It came at Prestwick in 1914 and Taylor did have his chance. He was two strokes ahead of Vardon moving into the final round. In his book *My Life's Work*, Taylor admits, "I do own up to being a bit flustered when we got to the tee to begin the last round. The Glasgow trains had disgorged their hundreds of passengers, the crowd was large and insatiable in its desire to push forward and see everything that was going on."

Taylor's putting, regarded then as perhaps the most consistent part of his game, let him down. He could not fight his way back after a seven at the fourth—Vardon took four—and his game suffered. Vardon finished with a 78 to Taylor's 83 and he won by three shots. It was a magnificent performance for it won him a record sixth Open Championship—a record which remains today although Tom Watson is poised to equal it after five wins himself.

So Vardon, with his famous grip, was able to grasp true immortality although an era of golf was, because of the war, to come to a natural conclusion. Braid, Taylor, and Vardon, The Great Triumvirate, returned to compete in the Open Championship following the war but they were no longer the force that they had been. The

intervening years had not only removed some of their sharpness, but the time gap had meant others had been able to improve.

The first player to take advantage of this opportunity was George Duncan. In one respect it seemed fair and proper as on many occasions before the war he had been compelled to play a supporting role to the Triumvirate.

Now his chance came, although at first he was under some pressure after opening with successive rounds of 80. In fact he is the last Open champion to have won the title with a round of 80 or more during the week. His win came after he finished in great style with scores

of 71 and 72. It was a historic Championship, the first to be held under the auspices of the Royal and Ancient.

The six clubs that hosted the Open Championship decided that the time had arrived to have just one ruling body. So the R. and A. assumed responsibility, although this shift in power coincided with another that provided a pill far more bitter to swallow as far as British professionals were concerned.

In 1921, there was a historic United States win, albeit by a Scottish immigrant American called Jock Hutchison, and the cherished silver claret jug was winging, or rather sailing, its way

Right: Walter Hagen won the Open Championship for a second time when he edged out Ernest Whitcombe at Hoylake in 1924— he returned to triumph again in 1928 and 1929.

across the Atlantic for the first time. In a play-off Hutchison beat Roger Wethered, the brother of that "Lady of Swing," the superb Joyce Wethered.

America's golfers were on the march. In 1922 the first strident steps into the new dominance of golf were taken by the irrepressible Walter Hagen, a man of flamboyant character, with his

Open Championship win at Royal St. George's, Sandwich. It was to be his first of four Championship titles in eight years. Arthur Hovers won in 1923, pushing Hagen into second place when for the first time the Open took place at Troon, but Britain failed to triumph again until Henry Cotton won in 1934.

Peacetime had brought a revolution. In the pre-war years golfers like Taylor and Vardon had taken their game to the United States. They were regarded as world class and the only title thought to reflect their stature was the Open Championship.

Now post-war America would take the lead.

Above: The Prince of Wales (later Edward VIII) watching the progress of the Runyan and Alliss match during the Ryder Cup at Southport and Ainsdale on June 12, 1933. He later presented the Cup to the Great Britain team.

THE PENDULUM SWINGS

Right: Walter J. Travis, a late arrival to the game who only began playing at the age of 36 years, astonished the golfing world by making the Atlantic crossing from the United States in 1904 to win the Amateur Championship at Royal St. George's, Sandwich that year. The "Old Man," as Travis was known, returned home to a hero's welcome.

On February 22, 1888, as has already been recounted, John Reid invited several friends to his home in Yonkers, New York. One of them was Robert Lockhart, an immigrant Scot who had obtained a supply of golf clubs and balls. They used the equipment to play on three rough holes in Reid's pasture.

That day golf was born in the United States. The lunch guests had enjoyed the afternoon, experimenting with Lockhart's clubs, and they were to meet for dinner shortly afterward. Then and there they decided to found the St. Andrew's Golf Club. Other clubs, too, came into being around that time and, although all elected to follow the rules of the Royal and Ancient Golf Club of St. Andrews, each club conducted its own tournaments.

To most Americans it can be fairly assumed the pastime of hitting a ball, and of trying to pot it into a hole no bigger than a tin can, was nothing short of an insane exercise. Moreover the sport had no grounding whatsoever. For instance the U.S. Amateur Championship was forced to change the date on which it took place in order to accommodate the America's Cup match at Newport, Rhode Island.

The game of golf was on shaky ground not only because it was foreign to the nation but also because of the internal conflicts already raging between the few clubs that were then in existence in the United States. For both the St. Andrew's and the Newport clubs had started competitions. Although good would eventually come from such difficulties with the formation of the United States Golf Association in 1894, these pioneers still faced enormous problems—best illustrated by the fact that Willie Dunn's name is excluded from most modern day record books dealing with the U.S. Open.

Dunn, if he was alive today, would claim that in 1894 he became the first U.S. Open champion. Dunn was small of stature—he stood only five feet six inches—but big in heart and his inventive skills are to be applauded. He was, later in life, to be one of the first players to experiment with steel shafts, inserting thin steel rods in split cane and lancewood shafts. Moreover, he invented a cone-shaped paper tee which would lead to the wooden tee, and later his pioneering efforts would lead to the introduction of indoor golf schools.

He had, in the early 1890s, met with socialite W.K. Vanderbilt. Vanderbilt invited Dunn to New York, and so this dapper young man, with a penchant for wearing fedoras, joined a band of Scots whose experience and enthusiasm were to spark a greater interest in the game among Americans.

What happened, then, in 1894 was that the St. Andrew's Club, which was staging its own competition, also decided to go one better—presumably to be one up on Newport—by simultaneously running an open championship for the professionals. Dunn won the $100 first prize and a gold medal which he wore with pride for the rest of his life.

Above: The first photo of golf in America, made at the St. Andrew's Golf Course at Yonkers, New York, in 1888. Pictured (left to right) are Harry Holbrook, A. Kinnan, John B. Upham, and John Reid.

Sadly for Dunn, and perhaps this explains why he is often excluded from the record books, it was only later in 1894, on December 22, that the United States Golf Association was formed. The rivalry between Newport and St. Andrew's was clearly not good for the game of golf so together with representatives from the Country Club of Boston, Chicago, and Shinnecock Hills they met in order to secure another American dream.

The formation of the U.S.G.A. put new life into golf in America. Golf in the United States would make tremendous progress even if at first the U.S. Open would be won mostly by immigrant Scots of mature ages. The 1895 winner was a 21-year-old Englishman called Horace Rawlins and the luckless Dunn filled the runner's-up

berth. So today, in most textbooks, Rawlins' name heads the list of U.S. Open winners.

Progress was swift—by 1900 there were 1,000 courses—and in keeping with their promotional instinct, the adventurous Americans enticed Harry Vardon, already three times British Open Champion, to the U.S. for a series of exhibition matches. The establishment of the Royal and Ancient had sired a lusty offspring in the form of the U.S.G.A. Vardon's tour brought the game to thousands of Americans and with the newly formed U.S.G.A. getting into its stride, the presence of this showman inspired many others all over the United States to play the game.

Vardon spread the word of golf wherever he played. Everyone loves a winner and Vardon had the panache and style to attract big galleries of spectators. Even the New York Stock Exchange closed their doors early when Vardon was giving an exhibition locally to save the embarrassment of too many employees offering excuses for taking the day off.

In between the exhibitions, when he was accompanied by his great friend and rival, J.H. Taylor, Vardon competed in the U.S. Open at Chicago. He won and Taylor was runner-up. It was typical of the times but Americans were not slow in progressing. They learned fast, simply by watching and appreciating the skills of master craftsmen like Vardon and Taylor.

After Vardon's win came the best of the Scottish settlers, Willie Anderson. He was a dour man from North Berwick and he shunned publicity, although he could not but help put himself in the public limelight because of his rare talent. Just how big this talent was can be gauged by the fact that many observers believe that in any era he would have been a true champion. Records often speak louder than words and Anderson's four U.S. Open wins have never been bettered although Bobby Jones, Ben Hogan, and Jack Nicklaus would later all equal it.

Anderson won first in 1901. Laurie Auchterlonie interrupted his reign by taking the title in 1902 but Anderson won the next three. Anderson, too, did much for his profession. In 1901 he was not amused when, just before the first round, an official at the Myopia Hunt Club in Hamilton, Massachusetts, informed the players that amateurs could eat in the dining room but the professionals would have to go to the kitchen. Anderson, not one to lose his temper, roared, "Na, na . . . we're na goin' t' eat in the kitchen."

The outcome was that a tent was erected in which the professionals could eat. This was not entirely satisfactory but the professionals had at least climbed a couple of rungs up the social ladder.

In truth, Americans, so keen to win, gave more of their time around the turn of the century to the amateurs. The reason, quite simply, was that there was a feeling that their amateurs could win whereas their professionals simply could not cope with the experienced British players. The surprise was that it took a player who had only taken up the game at the age of 36, to produce the result that would send shock waves rolling through the British game. For Walter J. Travis, an adopted son who had emigrated from Australia when he was six years old, crossed the Atlantic to win the British Amateur Championship in 1904 at Royal St. George's, Sandwich.

Born in Maldon, Victoria on January 10, 1862, Travis was to leave Australia long before the formation of the Royal Melbourne Club in 1891—probably the first concrete date for the start of golf in Australia, even if several previous efforts to start clubs had taken place both there and in New Zealand.

In the United States Travis was not taken by the game until, like many in that country, the end of the 1890s. He was, of course, a very late starter but he was unquestionably extremely talented. Proof came in 1900 when, at the age of 38 and only two years after he had taken up the game, Travis won the U.S. Amateur Championship. He was to win again in 1901 and 1903.

Now it was time to take on the British on their own soil. Travis borrowed a center-shafted Schenectady putter from an American spectator and with that in his hands he proved unbeatable on the greens. He went past one opponent after another. In the final he faced Ted Blackwell, a hot favorite who could hit the ball the proverbial country mile. But Travis's putting power was more than a match for the powerhouse giant's advantage off the tee—Travis took Blackwell by the handsome margin of four and three. This was almost tantamount to aggressive invasion. Walter was given a sour reception by the locals and the R. and A. even banned the center-shafted putter. That ban, of course, was later lifted.

Nevertheless, an American had come to the old country, the birthplace of the game, and he was taking home the amateur title—the game of golf was the beneficiary. The "Old Man" as Travis was nicknamed, returned to a hero's welcome and the United States rejoiced in the knowledge that they now possessed a true champion of the game. There was much more to come and the American public loved it.

Anderson, sadly, was to lose his U.S. Open crown in 1906 when Alex Smith won. Anderson was on the way to an early death. His death certificate in 1910 recorded that he had died of arteriosclerosis, although others suggested that it was a case of acute alcoholism. Certainly professional golfers at that time were reputed to be heavy drinkers.

In that year of 1910, however, emerged one John McDermott who was to have a profound effect on the American scene. He was a cocky youngster from Philadelphia who had risen from the caddie ranks with one fervent intention—he wanted to become the first homebred American to win the U.S. Open. He was the son of a mailman and his desire and determination were reflected by the fact that he neither drank nor smoked. Indeed he rarely missed Sunday mass.

McDermott had to be content with a share of the runner's-up spoils in 1910 after he was beaten in a play-off by Alex Smith. His confidence, however, had increased to such an extent that early in 1911 he challenged fellow Philadelphian professionals to $1000 head-to-head matches. He won three in succession although all subsequent efforts to arrange another match failed!

In the 1911 Open it was McDermott's turn. This time, at the age of 19, he won a three-man play-off. Thus American golf had received the ultimate boost. The long wait was over. A born-and-bred American had won the U.S. Open. It was all that was needed to give impetus to the growing flame, kindled by Travis's Amateur Championship win in Sandwich, which would blaze a new-born hope of golfing glory across the length and breadth of America. For now the game was as popular on the west coast as it was on the east. McDermott won again in 1912 and his two wins started a sequence when "outsiders" simply were not allowed to win the U.S. Open. Ted Ray did in 1920 but, that apart, it was not until Gary Player of South Africa took the title in 1965 that another overseas player won.

McDermott was tipped to complete the hat-trick at The Country Club, Brookline, Massachusetts, although there he faced the ultimate challenge. Harry Vardon was back for a second sponsored tour, this time organized by newspaper baron Lord Northcliffe. Along with Vardon came Ted Ray who had won the British Open in 1912 with Vardon runner-up. Vardon and Ray, who played with his pipe sticking out of his mouth, invariably attracted large audiences wherever they appeared.

But the tide of fortune was turning. While on that tour Ray and Vardon were to take in the U.S.

Open. McDermott was waiting for them but among the chasers there was also a 20-year-old local lad called Francis Ouimet and a teenage upstart from New York called Walter Hagen. Ouimet's golfing education stemmed from playing on some rough holes carved in the backyard of his Boston home. Even so he had already hinted at his prowess by reaching the semifinals of the U.S. Amateur Championship. The kid, however, had ambition and as the Massachusetts champion he was quite prepared to take on such great players as McDermott, Ray, and Vardon.

McDermott was not to figure this time but Ray and Vardon, each of whom led their qualify-

Right: Outstanding golfer and popular personality, Walter Hagen plays from the 10th tee at Troon during the 1923 Open Championship. Hagen finished runner-up, one shot behind Arthur Havers.

ing sections, were there. They posted their scores of 304, leaving Ouimet at that time to play the last eight holes in one under par for a 79 to match the totals of the two British golfers. Ouimet heard a spectator talking about him: "It's too bad but he's blown up," he said.

Ouimet was inspired by the remark. He vowed to himself and to his ten-year-old caddie, Eddie Lowery, that he would at least force his way into the play-off. He did so with a birdie at the 17th, holing from 15 feet, and a par at the last where he confidently holed from a distance of four feet.

The local hero and office clerk playing in his own backyard was taking on the formidable British pair in no uncertain style in a play-off that smacked of high drama. This unassuming young-ster, an amateur, the epitome of American youth, seemed out of his class.

Yet like a story from a boys' adventure book there had to be a magic ending. McDermott pat-ted Ouimet on the back before the start, whis-pering, "You're hitting the ball well—now go out and play your own game," and out Ouimet went in the misty rain with 10,000 spectators watching avidly.

Out he went, in fact, to make the tale come true. He overcame the famous British duo with a 72 to Vardon's 77 and Ray's 78. Vardon, it is said, was seen smoking a cigarette on the course for

the first time in his career. Ray drew anxiously on his pipe throughout the game. Ouimet might have said to them afterward, "Put that in your pipe and smoke it!" Instead, at the prize-giving he simply said, "Naturally it was always my hope to win out. I simply tried my best to keep this cup from going to our friends from across the water. I am very glad to have been the agency for keeping the cup in America."

Sport, no less than any other activity, needs a hero. Better still if that hero has qualifications, like Ouimet's amateur status. Ouimet's victory was that of a small man overcoming the giants, the American Dream come true. There can be little doubt that this almost no-hoper fired the imagi-nation of those who aspired to achieve against the odds. He had set American golf onto the "Fairways of Fortune."

America would be roused into producing perhaps the finest exponents of this Scottish-born game, with others following the lead set first by Travis, then McDermott, and then Ouimet. Players of no mean ability were to come forward, possessing that little something else—personality and star quality. Walter Hagen fitted that bill to a tee. He was the streetwise kid from Rochester, New York, the indomitable predator of the fairways. Hagen would make bold predic-tions—and he delivered them. Hagen had missed a chance in 1913 and had fallen by the wayside.

LEFT: John G. Anderson (left) and
Jerome D. Travers, the runner-up and
winner respectively, of the U.S.
Amateur Championship in 1913.

At first he was against playing in 1914 at the
Midlothian Country Club at Blue Island, Illinois.
But a sponsor came in to pay Hagen's fare to
Chicago. He took with him the same outfit that
he had worn the previous year. This sartorial outfit consisted of white flannels, with the cuff
turned up just once, a loud striped silk shirt and
a red bandanna which he knotted around his

neck. He did leave behind the white buckskin shoes with rubber soles, because at Brookline he had slipped on the wet turf. Instead he wore shoes with hobnails protruding from the soles which offered extra grip just like spikes would later on.

That outfit said much for the man. And the dashing, flashing Walter won in style, too, with a score of 290. Between them McDermott, Ouimet, and Hagen had sent the ball flying for American golf. They were men of exceptional character, charged with the desire to promote the game in the best interests of the professional. Barred from using golf club changing rooms, they hired a limousine in which to change and in which to eat. Hagen, above all, helped to change that insensate outlook.

Ouimet was held in such high regard that the R. and A. bestowed upon him the exceptional honor in 1957 of appointing him the first non-British captain. He had visited Britain with Jerome Travers, another American amateur who won the U.S. Open in 1915, to compete in the Amateur Championship after the war. So fancied were these two golfers that one daring individual wagered that one of the two would take the British title and he placed a bet of £10,000 at 3-1. However Ouimet and Travers would soon lose their position in the rankings.

Hagen was a very different character from Ouimet. But together the pair inspired more homebred winners, with Charles Evans Junior, another amateur, taking the U.S. Open in 1916 before the war halted play in 1917 and 1918.

But the irrepressible Hagen was back on the scene at Brae Burn, West Newton, Massachusetts, to win in 1919 following a play-off with Mike Brady.

The U.S. title, perhaps fittingly, fell to Ted Ray, that old campaigner of the prewar days who had lost in the 1913 play-off to Ouimet, in 1920. He was, however, to be the last in the line of foreign winners until South Africa's Gary Player won in 1965.

By now golf in the United States was in full swing. There had been an air of indifference about the future of the sport. But the Roaring Twenties and the likes of Walter Hagen and Bobby Jones would alter all that. America was ready to launch into a period of expansion, the likes of which had never been seen before. That left the rest of the world behind as golf in the United States rode high on this bandwagon of euphoria.

The growing wealth of the nation, of course, was as much a spur as anything else. Henry Ford's legendary Model-T epitomized the foresight and inspiration among Americans. Aviation was producing pioneers such as Amelia Earhart and Charles Lindbergh, while sporting stars such as baseball idol "Babe" Ruth were becoming huge celebrities. The game of golf would share in this new surging, headlong advance.

The spirit of enterprise could be seen in the progress of club manufacture and equipment too. America immediately seized this opportunity to gain a large slice of the market. There was money to be made in clubs and balls. Interest in the game had risen to such a degree that the U.S. Professional Golfers' Association had been formed in 1916 and with that had come the U.S. P.G.A. Championship. The U.S. P.G.A. first sprang to life following a lunch during which Rodman Wanamaker, the son of a Philadelphia department store owner, suggested to the party, which consisted mostly of professionals, that the time was ripe for a U.S. P.G.A. Championship. The

Above: Jim Barnes waits to be presented with his trophy for winning the Open Championship in 1925, while the Captain of the Prestwick Club delivers his speech.

Championship started life as a set of knock-out matches (match-play), only changing from that format to stroke-play (player with fewest strokes over the tounament wins) in 1958, and, of course, amateurs were not eligible.

Like most early competitions it would take a few years for an American champion to emerge. But in 1921 Walter Hagen won the first of his five P.G.A. titles in seven years—a sequence broken only by Gene Sarazen's wins in 1922 and 1923. More importantly the U.S. P.G.A. Championship went to new courses, so spreading the gospel of golf, and there were new winners, like Leo Diegel in 1928 and 1929, Tommy Armour in 1930, Tom Creavy in 1931, and Olin Dutra in 1932, who would promote the competition.

But it was Hagen's impeccable performances in those years that did so much for the sport. He was setting the pace in terms of appearance money for exhibition matches with such style that his fellow professionals could have no qualms as the prize stakes for the tournaments grew. Now, almost overnight, Hagen was to transport his skills to Britain. It was the start of the revolution. American golf had forged ahead to the point where it could directly challenge Britain. Now Hagen was to lead the way for Americans to monopolize the Open Championship.

True, Arthur Havers won it in 1923 but Hagen scored again in 1924. Then came Jim Barnes (1925), Bobby Jones (1926, 1927, and 1930), Hagen again in 1928 and 1929, Tommy

Armour in 1931, Gene Sarazen in 1932, and Denny Shute in 1933.

Yet with his colorful personality and what he brought to the game, Hagen was to blow away some of the cobwebs of predictability and dullness and instead add the appeal that exists today. His bright golfing wear and lighthearted humor made him very popular and increased the galleries wherever he played.

Hagen might have crossed swords with official-dom more often than he cared to remember, but he roared throughout the twenties. His butler would serve him champagne and oysters from the trunk of his chauffeur-driven limousine. Nicknamed "The Haig" he would play in silk shirts with monograms and two-tone shoes. His trademarks, too, were handmade suits and solid gold cuff links. He lived life to the full and he never forgot his own words, "So many people today never have time to stop off and smell the flowers as they go through life."

The British, of course, were not too pleased with the annual loss of a piece of their sporting heritage. They were not exactly happy with this "invasion" by American golfers and they frowned upon a certain K.T. Jones, Junior, who had the audacity to tear up his card at the short 11th in 1921 when he played in the Open Championship at St. Andrews for the first time. Jones was to regret this rash act for years. Even so he was to be forgiven by the people of Britain, for Bobby Jones, as he is better known, not only learned

Above: Gene Sarazen of the United States drives off from the first tee during the Open Championship at Hoylake, Royal Liverpool, in 1924. Sarazen finished way down the field, behind Walter Hagen, but he was to win the title at Prince's, Sandwich, in 1932.

Above: Bobby Jones with the Open Championship trophy—the silver claret jug—he won in 1926 at Royal Lytham and St Annes. The American amateur returned to win in 1927 and 1930.

from that incident but became arguably the greatest golfer in the history of the game.

Robert Tyre Jones was born in Atlanta, Georgia on March 17, 1902. The new breed of American Open champions in that rise of supremacy led first by McDermott, Ouimet, and Hagen, and subsequently followed by Jim Barnes (1921) and Gene Sarazen (1922), was continued by Jones. Here was a man whose hallmark really was perfection.

Jones's charming manner on and off the course was almost sufficient to persuade people in the United States and Britain alike to hand the trophies over to him. And he could charm the ball with equal flair and his triple winning of the Open Championship in 1926, 1927, and 1930 should have been glory enough. His record included a memorable win in the U.S. Open at Inwood, New York, in 1923, following a play-off with Bobby Cruickshank. He was, of

course, to crown his achievements in 1930 by completing the Grand Slam of golf, winning the U.S. Open, the U.S. Amateur, and the British equivalents all within the same year. Just for the record he shares with Ben Hogan, Jack Nicklaus, and Willie Anderson the record of four U.S. Open triumphs. He won his in 1923, 1926, 1929, and 1930 and he was runner-up after play-offs against W. MacFarlane in 1925 and Johnny Farrell in 1928, and second, too, to Sarazen in 1922 and

Cyril Walker in 1924. Jones was U.S. Amateur champion in 1924, 1925, 1927, 1928, and 1930 apart from being runner-up in 1919 and 1926.

These are just a few of the major honors that Jones won. There was a great deal more to the man than simply these cups and trophies, and his achievements seem all the more impressive when one remembers the unlikely beginnings of his career. For instance Jones, or so it is claimed by some observers, was a weedy youngster with

Above: Bobby Jones drives from the 17th tee during the Open Championship at St Andrews in 1927 when he successfully defended his title with a record score of 285. He won by six shots from Aubrey Boomer and Fred Robson.

57

Above: A group picture taken prior to the Open Championship at Muirfield in 1929 where Walter Hagen (front row, second from the left) won the trophy for the fourth time in eight years.

a shyness that had a self-destructive component. That apart, he had plenty of heart. And when his father, a lawyer, moved home from Atlanta, young Bobby had the chance to prove himself at a new club—the East Lake Country Club. On that course—as at many others in America—there was a Scottish professional. In this case it was Stewart Maiden from Carnoustie, and Bobby spent many hours at his side, using a trimmed shaft to develop the most natural of swings.

In truth Jones was able to reach the top because of his sheer measured talent. The road, undoubtedly, was tough, given the nature of the young man, but when he finally overcame his nervousness it was to reach greatness of a level which,

perhaps, in the history of the game only Jack Nicklaus can be said to have equaled. Yet it is a fact that Jones, a keen scholar who gained a first class honors degree in law, was such a nervous player that he was frequently physically sick during championships—something few people realised at the time. With his stylish, rhythmical swing he was admired by all, but because of his nervousness he was still often unable to eat during championships.

Yet no one who knew the man would deny that in Bobby Jones was a person, a player, to inspire others. He had everything from ability to integrity to sportsmanship. If anyone ever ditched the theory about nice guys never making it then Robert Tyre Jones did and in no uncertain style.

He was the one who raised the status of the U.S. Open, making it the most important golfing tournament to win.

Jones had, in short, gained the love of everybody in the game. If an example is required then recall how in 1936, on his way to the Olympic Games, he stopped en route at St. Andrews. There was not a soul in sight when Jones stood on the first tee, firing his opening drive down that wide expanse of fairway, nor was there as he approached the green. But the word was soon spread around the "auld grey toon" that Bobby Jones was there. And by the second hole 2,000 people had joined him! He was to return again in 1958, as the non-playing captain of the United States Eisenhower team, and St. Andrews bestowed upon this much-loved man The Freedom of the Burgh. This was no lightweight honor since the last American previously accorded that distinction was none other than Benjamin Franklin.

Scotland never forgets its heroes. "Wee Bobby's" popularity was legendary, and in 1927 he was carried off the last green after he had shot a record aggregate score of 285—pushing Aubrey Boomer into second place—setting not only a new low for the Championship but a total in the Open for St. Andrews which would stand until 1955. In 1958 Jones summed up his affection for St. Andrews, saying, "I could take out of my life

Above: From left to right are P. E. Leviton, Olin Dutra, Billy Burke, Walter Hagen and Al Free, at Gleneagles, Perthshire, prior to the Open at St. Andrews in 1933.

Right: Walter Hagan leaves the last green at Muirfield, where he won the Open in 1929. He is being congratulated by Henry Cotton.

everything except my experiences at St. Andrews and I'd still have a rich, full life." The whole assembly rose, in a spontaneous and emotional tribute, and sang to their dear friend, "Will ye n'a come back again?"

Jones, who died in 1971 after many years of suffering with a crippling spinal disease, left his monument to the game. For it was back in Atlanta, after he had settled on a legal career, that he developed the idea of staging a tournament of his own. It was, of course, the U.S. Masters and it has been played at Augusta, Georgia, since 1934. Initially it took place in March to accommodate the newspaper sportswriters who were traveling home following the annual springtime pilgrimage

to Florida for the start of the baseball season. Jones, following his Grand Slam in 1930, had retired at the age of 28. Business interests came first but, with golf in his blood, Jones wanted a place where he could play with his friends and he found it some 100 miles away from his Atlanta home. It was a nursery known as "Fruitlands" and the 365 acres were for sale at depression prices. The financing was not a problem because Jones had been befriended by Clifford Roberts, a New York investor who was quite willing to become involved as he, too, wanted a secluded place to play golf with his friends.

So, with the assistance of Dr. Alister Mackenzie, a Scottish physician turned golf

course architect, Jones and Roberts brought to life one of the great shrines of the game. They created a masterpiece at Augusta which became the perfect, permanent site for the U.S. Masters. Jones, of course, had never visualized the Masters becoming the important event it is today. That, however, is what the sportswriters of the time insisted on calling it.

Now the United States not only had the world's greatest golfers but also they had three great championships—the U.S. Open, the U.S. Masters, and the U.S. P.G.A. Championship. The power of the British players had sagged and it was now their turn to go west in search of golfing greatness.

Henry Cotton recalls, "I thought that if I was ever going to be a good player I had better go to America and see just how they set about the game."

It was an astonishing statement although one that could be supported by the results in the Open Championship alone. There had been 12 years of autonomous American control and it seemed destined to go on forever. Then in 1934 Cotton was rewarded for his thoughtful endeavors. He won the Open at Royal St. George's. Britain had found a very worthy champion to end this dominance by the United States.

Above: Walter Hagen escapes from a bunker during the 1923 Open Championship at Troon.

Right: Bobby Jones retired in 1930 but he returned to competitive golf in 1934 in order to compete in the first U.S. Masters on the course which he had built at Augusta. He teed off on March 22, 1934, and he took 76 shots to play 18 holes, but for Jones it was the playing, rather than the winning, that had by this time become more important to him.

Above: Smiling happily, the proud possessor of the Open title, Bobby Jones (center) arrives in New York on the S.S. *Aquitania* accompanied by Al Watrous (left) and Walter Hagen (right). He was greeted by a delegation from his home town of Atlanta as well as a huge crowd of New Yorkers, besides being accorded an official welcome.

THE GOLDEN YEARS

Right: Walter Hagen (right) and his opponent, Percy Alliss, at Wannsee, Berlin.

In 1934 the inaugural U.S. Masters was won by Horton Smith, the U.S. Open by Olin Dutra, the U.S. P.G.A. Championship by Paul Runyan and the Open Championship by Henry Cotton. Two important milestones had been reached: the birth of the U.S. Masters, which was a watershed in American golf, and Cotton's success at Royal St. George's, Sandwich, which would earn him the admiration of the British public.

That was natural enough since Britain had been starved of a home winner of their very own Open title for 12 years. Cotton opened with a 67 and he followed this with a record round of 65. That score was to inspire a name—the Dunlop 65 golf ball—but more importantly it gave its maker a seven-shot lead. A third round of 72 stretched the advantage to nine.

Cotton was now home and dry . . . or so he thought.

The game of golf, however, is littered with stories of sudden U-turns by players psychologically destroyed by the special pressures associated with leadership. The slightest deviation from the norm can trigger a traumatic response. So it was for Cotton as, on reaching the first tee with five minutes, or so he thought, before the start of the final round, he was informed that there would be a 15-minute delay. The stewards required more time to organize the enormous crowd of spectators. Cotton was totally unprepared for this delay. He sat alone in an empty tent with his stomach churning. It has

been suggested that Cotton ate too much ice cream or spaghetti. Nothing could be farther from the truth. In those days two rounds were played in one day and, following his 72 in the morning, Cotton had sat down to a light lunch. It was sufficient to sustain him but as he was on a strict diet he did not overindulge. The trouble for Cotton was that he had a delicate stomach and the delay simply activated his anxiety and this in turn brought on an excruciating stomach cramp.

He struggled to the turn in 40. Fortunately he had begun with an appreciable advantage and he managed to hole from ten feet at the 13th to avoid marking a fourth successive five on his card. Cotton held on and the Open title remained in British hands.

Now Cotton, armed with the experience of touring America, could transform the game in Britain. However Hagen, responsible with Jones for turning the tide of fortune in America's favor during the twenties, would detonate Cotton's desire. On his 1928 trip to America, Cotton began to realize that golf was indeed a golden game paying golden dollars. Hagen was not only smelling the flowers but he was making a mint along the way, earning thousands of dollars from exhibition matches. Cotton would later recall: "He was the man who made me think. I was impressed by his way of life and I wanted to be like him."

The British scene, too, needed revitalizing. Cotton, a former public schoolboy, possessed the

Above: Glory for Henry Cotton (right) at Royal St. George's, where, following the victory in the Open Championship, he was presented with the trophy by Michael Scott, captain of the Sandwich club.

inspiration and the intelligence to do that. He was well versed in the eccentricities of the middle class. By demanding, and in many cases obtaining, increased prize funds he set new standards. Furthermore, he disturbed some golf officials, in particular the French, by telling them in no uncertain terms that the only way to

get the best players was to pay the best price for them.

And Cotton was the best. Like it or not, his style, on and off the fairways, proved a winner. He could charm the birds from the trees. He became so celebrated that he was often invited to top the bill at certain theaters with a performance of

Left: Sam Snead outside the clubhouse at St. Andrews, during the 1946 Open Championship, which he won. Considered to be one of the best golfers of all time, Snead won every major golf tournament during his 40 year career, except for the U.S. Open, which he lost by only one stroke in 1949.

trick shots. This, then, was the era in which Cotton dominated in Britain. He was to win the Open again in 1937, a victory in which there was much merit as many of the leading American golfers were present, and in 1948 following the Second World War.

This was the time, too, of the Great Depression and it is fair to reflect that although Britain regained individual control of the Open leading up to the war years of 1939 to 1945, this was only because Americans suddenly turned their backs on the championship. One could cite the cost of crossing the Atlantic as a reason, or the birth of the U.S. Masters in 1934.

In fact there was no time clash, as the Masters was to be played in March, and then later on in April, and the Open in July, but it did offer Americans another important championship in which to play. The Great Depression might have been hanging over the United States, but there was no stopping the expansion of golf. The depression, however, had spread globally so that the British contingent at the first Masters was not exactly what Jones would have liked or expected.

The winner, however, was well known to Cotton. Horton Smith, a lanky lad from Missouri with imposing good looks, had won 11 of the 17 tournaments in which Cotton had played during his tour of America in the winter of 1928–29. It was an impressive record considering the presence of players like Tommy Armour, Craig Wood, and Walter Hagen. Smith and Hagen, however, were like chalk and cheese, which showed in the different way they approached a game.

Smith would resist all temptations. He stuck rigidly to a milk-drinking diet and he enjoyed nothing more than going to bed early. Cotton, in his book *This Game of Golf*, tells the story of how at one golf club function Smith sat next to a pretty, sophisticated woman who offered him a cigarette. Smith, a non-smoker, refused. "Don't you drink either?" To that Smith replied, "No!" "Then you have no vices?" came the next question. Smith, with a twinkle in his eye, said, "Oh yes, I have. I'm often short with my long putts!" As Cotton recalls of this incident, there was a lull in the conversation at that juncture.

Smith was a superb putter and the marvelous greens which Jones built at Augusta National were made for him. He took full advantage by winning in 1934 and then again in 1936. The one nagging disappointment for Jones in 1934 had been the absence of Gene Sarazen. Sarazen had, in 1933, won the U.S. P.G.A. Championship for a third time to add to his two U.S. Opens and one British Open. He had subsequently committed himself to an exhibition tour through South America where the game had initially been transported by British golf enthusiasts employed to help build a railroad network in Argentina. The Buenos Aires Club had been formed in 1878, and with railroads encouraging travel and so spreading the golf bug, in 1890 another club was established at São Paulo, Brazil.

Sarazen was helping to promote the game although he had promised Jones, a close friend, that he would be at Augusta in 1935. At the time Sarazen was regarded as the leading player in the world, but not even this son of an immigrant carpenter from Italy could have predicted the stroke of brilliance he would execute in order to win the second U.S. Masters. It was a stroke that would be marveled at around the world and which, unquestionably, put the U.S. Masters firmly on the map.

Craig Wood, the runner-up the previous year, was back in the clubhouse with his score on the board. He had birdied the last hole and on hearing the roar of the crowd Walter Hagen, then 42 and Sarazen's partner that final round, turned to him and declared, "I think we can say that it is all over now." He knew that Sarazen would need three birdies in the last four holes to tie with Wood.

Sarazen was in the middle of the fairway at the 15th, a par five. As he pulled his fairway wood from the bag, ambitiously electing to go for the green guarded at the front by a creek, so Jones joined a dozen or so spectators near the putting green. The ball fizzed through the air. It caught the far bank of the water hazard but kicked on. It bounced a couple of times then, softly, and to the amazement of those privileged to see it, toppled into the hole. Sarazen had made an albatross, or a double-eagle, and that alone was sufficient for him to tie with Wood.

It was a winning blow in more ways than one. Wood, shattered by the shot, lost the play-off to Sarazen who had the psychological advantage. More importantly, the shot helped to breathe life into the game. The great crash of 1929 had jolted the American population who needed their golfing ambition to be rekindled. It was 1,000,000-1 shots like the one struck by Sarazen that helped to inspire them. Everybody needs a slice of good fortune in life and if it could happen on the fairways of Augusta then it could happen anywhere.

Smith too would enjoy a touch of luck in 1936 by holing a 50-foot chip during the final round at the 14th hole to give him his second victory. By then much was happening with the U.S. Tour which had managed to survive the depression. For instance in 1930 the St. Paul

Junior Chamber of Commerce had raised $10,000 in order to stage a tournament the week following the U.S. Open. And Bob Harlow, who for years had managed the incomparable Walter Hagen, was charged with beefing up the image of the game to make it more attractive to sponsors and spectators alike. It was an Everest-like challenge in the sunken economic climate, but with the advent of steel shafts came better equipment and lower scores. It was easier to "sell" an improving sport and players were now breaking 70 regularly. That made better reading.

The U.S. Tour incorporated approximately 15 tournaments with the leading money winner earning in the region of $7,000. During the depression, when one in four working adults were unemployed, that, too, made pretty good reading. Even so, not everyone was happy and that included George Jacobus who at the time was the president of the P.G.A. of America.

Harlow was involved in promoting exhibitions in which players like Hagen, whom he had managed, participated and he also wrote a syndicated golf column. In short some people questioned Harlow's motives at times and some professionals felt a certain section was receiving a rough deal. Jacobus grasped the nettle. He removed Harlow from the position of tournament manager and he also asked Horton Smith, a close friend of Harlow, to vacate his position as chairman of the tournament committee. Sparks flew with the appointment of Fred Corcoran, an Irishman who lived in Boston and was at the time working for the Massachusetts Golf Association.

Corcoran was paid a salary of $5,000 and was worth every cent. He transformed the scene by raising the prize fund in two years by $60,000 and in 1938 the professionals played a 20-strong

Left: American Gene Sarazen helps his wife to practice her swing on the deck of the S.S. *Mauretania* as they arrive in Britain.

71

tournament circuit for $160,000. In his efforts Corcoran was undoubtedly helped by the arrival of Sam Snead. The tour needed a breath of fresh air and Snead, from White Sulphur Springs, West Virginia, provided that from the moment he played his first practice round with four well-dressed, experienced professionals. Snead stood on the first tee in a long-sleeved white shirt and a pair of baggy pants. He hit his first two drives out of bounds, topped his next into a pond and, on being cajoled into reloading again, slammed his next effort onto the green—345 yards away! So Snead, a bundle of fun and possessing the strength of an ox, became "Slamming Sam." And the Tour had a star to help to promote its wares.

Not that the "old guard" had quite disappeared. Sarazen's crowning glory had come at Augusta in 1935, but in 1940 he was still on the scene when

Left: Photographed on the first tee at Philadelphia G.C. where the U.S. Open was held in 1939 are (left to right) Craig Wood, Denny Shute, and Byron Nelson before the start of a three-way play-off which Nelson won.

Right: Denny Shute playing in the
P.G.A. tourney at Pittsburgh,
Pennsylvania in 1937.

he was edged out in a play-off for the U.S. Open at Canterbury, Ohio. His rival was Lawson Little and the tournament came no less than 18 years after Sarazen had won the Championship. Meanwhile Craig Wood, the man whom Sarazen had managed to destroy with his albatross two in the U.S. Masters, eventually lost his unenviable tag as the "nearly man" of golf.

A potted history of Wood's misfortunes would read like a killing field had all not come to a glorious end when through sheer determination he eventually triumphed. In describing his trials and tribulations it is worth recalling that in 1933 he finished third in the U.S. Open then lost the Open Championship to compatriot Denny Shute following an exciting 36-hole play-off at St. Andrews.

Wood was punished at St Andrews by his big hitting, which on several occasions meant he drove himself into trouble, and it also put Wood on a run of more misses. He was runner-up in each of the first two U.S. Masters. Another blow was dealt to him at the Park Country Club, Williamsville, New York, in 1934, where he was beaten at the 38th hole by Paul Runyan in the final of the U.S. P.G.A. Championship.

Still the kicks kept coming. In the 1939 U.S. Open he tied both with Byron Nelson who had made his presence felt by winning the 1937 U.S. Masters, and Denny Shute. Shute went out after the first of the two play-off rounds at the Philadelphia Country Club, but Wood was still matching Nelson stroke for stroke after 36 holes. When they moved onto extra holes Nelson holed a full one iron—shades of Sarazen and Augusta 1935! Champions, however, never quit. And luck was about to change quite dramatically for this indefatigable character.

Wood had determined that the 1941 U.S. Masters would be his, although his doubts must have been roused when after being five shots up he saw his lead being whittled away as Nelson swept to the turn in 33 compared to his own 38. This time his never-say-die attitude helped Wood to birdies at the 13th, 15th, and 16th holes, and he was home. Life's succession of ups and downs was at last turning for Craig in the kindest possible way. That same year he won the U.S. Open at the Colonial Country Club in Fort Worth, Texas. Ironically he considered withdrawing on the eve of the Championship because of that most perennial of problems to a golfer—a bad back. Craig, however, strapped himself up and he battled to a three-stroke win over his old adversary, Denny Shute. The "nearly man" had at last got there.

At this point the war intervened. The U.S. Open would not be played again until 1946 when Lloyd Mangrum would emerge as the winner at the Canterbury Golf Club, Cleveland, Ohio. The U.S. Masters, however, was played in 1942, with Byron Nelson winning, and that same year the U.S. P.G.A. Championship unfolded at the Seaview Country Club, Atlantic City, New Jersey, with Snead the winner. Yet with the war ending, there was a new era dawning. This new era had been ushered in by Nelson and Snead and the tournament scene in the States flourished with the arrival, too, of Jimmy Demaret and Ben Hogan.

Samuel Jackson Snead, born in Hot Springs, Virginia on May 27, 1912, was destined never to win the U.S. Open. He did, however, win the Open Championship at St. Andrews in 1946. The United States had bypassed this, the oldest and most prestigious of championships, during the immediate prewar years. In addition to Cotton,

Far Left: Lloyd Mangrum drives from the first tee in the opening round of the 30th annual Los Angeles Open. Mangrum finished first in the 72 hole contest carding a record low of 272.

Left: Sam Snead hones his game on the practice range in 1956 while watched by his son, Sam Junior.

Alf Perry (1935), Alf Padgham (1936), R.A. Whitcombe (1938), and Richard Burton (1939) had stepped in to win. More than 200 players, however, entered in 1946 and this proved the first real sign of the game's move toward becoming a truly international sport, for Bobby Locke of South Africa and Norman von Nida of Australia were among the many entrants.

Although Locke had played in Britain before, it was only after the war that he was to make his presence felt. Snead, however, was made the hot favorite and he won by four strokes, albeit with a little assistance from an official. Snead heard that one of his pitching clubs was likely to be singled out for inspection—the R. and A. had been told that certain American professionals were in the habit of roughing up the faces of their clubs—and

so he asked a member of the Championship Committee for permission to use the club in question. It is said that he owed his homeward 35 to being able to use this club to stop the ball downwind on the lightning-fast greens.

Snead, however, was a fine golfer and his record reflects that. He not only won both the U.S. Masters (1949, 1952, and 1954) and U.S. P.G.A. Championship (1942, 1949, and 1951) on three occasions each but he is also credited with having scored no fewer than 135 victories. No less than 81—a record—of those came on the U.S. P.G.A. Tour, his first being the 1936 West Virginia P.G.A. closed event and his last the Greensboro Open in 1965. He did become a victim of the putting yips although he devised a unique method to conquer them. Originally he

Above: Byron Nelson "Mr. Golf" with his caddy on the ninth green of the Pomonok Country Club course after Nelson won his match with Emerick Kocsis in the quarter finals of the 1939 U.S. P.G.A. Championship. Nelson lost in the final to Henry Picard.

started to putt, croquet-style, between his legs but when that was banned he resorted to standing with both feet together, facing the hole and with the ball ahead of his right toe.

Byron Nelson, who became known as "Mr. Golf," had an ideal golfing temperament, being a methodical person with a good brain. His mechanical style is best illustrated by his record in 1945 when he won 11 consecutive events and a total of 18 in a single calendar year. For good measure he also won two U.S. Masters, two U.S. P.G.A. Championships, and one U.S. Open. He was, however, to depart the scene early, seeking a quieter life because the high tension of professional golf did not suit his nervous stomach.

The likes of Jimmy Demaret, three times U.S. Masters champion, galvanized the game. He was one of those gifted players who could sail along effortlessly without spending much time on the practice range. He had talent, sackfuls of the stuff, and a brilliant putting touch. He also had style. When he won his second U.S. Masters in 1947 he dressed on Sunday like a canary with a bright yellow outfit. "If you're going to be in the limelight then you might as well dress for it," he said.

American golf, too, had come into the public limelight in 1947 when at the U.S. Open at St. Louis Country Club in Missouri a television

camera was placed behind the 18th green. The prize fund that year was $10,000—the first time a five-figure amount was at stake—but the presence of television, albeit just the one camera serving less than 1,000 sets in St. Louis, was to trigger a revolution. The message of golf would be relayed to watching millions because of a shot that owed as much to fortune as it did to skill.

George May, an eccentric millionaire, had backed a new event, the World Championship of Golf. The World, as it became known, grew in stature as the prize money increased, from $35,000 in 1949 to $75,000 in 1953. Lew Worsham, who had won the U.S. Open in 1947,

came to the last needing a birdie to tie with Chandler Harper, the 1950 U.S. P.G.A. champion. Instead those watching millions saw Harper scoop the $25,000 first prize, as well as some lucrative contracts, when he succeeded in holing a wedge shot for an unlikely eagle two.

The public, coast to coast, were bewitched then, and again that summer by Hogan at the Open Championship at Carnoustie. Here was a legendary figure, whom some would consider to be the greatest golfer of all, although supporters of Jones and Nicklaus would argue with that.

Hogan had been a professional since 1931 ,but he had been around courses as an 11-year-

Above: Sam Snead in action during the 1953 Ryder Cup at Wentworth, England.

Far Left: Past masters Sam Snead
and Gene Sarazen (left) shake hands
at the 1996 U.S. Masters in Augusta.

Left: Proving that he hasn't lost his
touch Sam Snead plays from a
bunker during the "Legends of Golf"
tournament in 1996.

Right: Ben Hogan playing in the Canada Cup in 1956 at Wentworth in Surrey, England, where he partnered Sam Snead to victory for the United States.

Below Right: Some of the United States Ryder Cup team pictured soon after their arrival in London in September 1953 for the biennial encounter with Great Britain. They are (left to right): Lloyd Mangrum, Dr. Cary Middlecoff, Ed Oliver, Sam Snead, Jim Turnesa, Jack Burke, Walter Burkemo, and Ted Kroll with traveling companions Harry F. Radix, Joe Jemsek, Roy O'Brien and manager Fred Corcoran.

old caddying at his home town club of Dublin, Texas. He had taken the top money spot on the U.S. Tour in 1940 and, after the war years, he came back with a flourish by winning five tournaments in 1945.

However, he craved the "majors," the title given to the U.S. Masters, U.S. Open, U.S. P.G.A. Championship, and the Open Championship, and it was not until 1946 that he broke through into that league when he won the U.S. P.G.A. Championship by beating Ed Oliver six and four in the final at Portland, Oregon. Hogan was to win the P.G.A. title again, whipping Mike Turnesa seven and six in the 1948 final at Norwood Hills, St. Louis, and he eclipsed that with his victory in the U.S. Open also that year at the Riviera Country Club in Los Angeles. Most observers regarded Hogan as the best in the world at that time—he had already been leading money winner on the Tour on four occasions and had taken the Vardon Trophy for the lowest scoring average no fewer than three times but this victory was the final proof.

It could also have been Hogan's final input to the game and to life. He slumped into his Cadillac, exhausted by the ordeal of winning, and turned to his wife Valerie. "Let's go home," he said. "I'm tired. I want to die an old man, not a young one." So they set off to drive back to Fort Worth, Texas. The night was thick with a ghostly fog and as Hogan drove slowly into a small town called Van Horn he saw two headlamps emerge from the darkness. It was too late. There was a sickening crash. Hogan flung his body across his wife, protecting her, and in so doing he almost certainly saved his own life. For afterward investigators found that the steering column had speared the driver's seat.

Some feared he would never walk again. Golf was out of the question. Hogan had a double fracture of the pelvis. He had broken his left ankle, his collarbone and just about every rib in his body. His left knee too was badly damaged. As Hogan lay on his back for two months so the sport appeared to have lost a hero in his prime.

Hogan, however, would not allow his injuries to deter him. He even posted his entry for the U.S. Open in 1949. He did not make that event but he was, miraculously, at Merion in 1950. There Hogan displayed all the courageous fighting spirit that had helped to restore him to top-flight tournament golf.

He had tied with Lloyd Mangrum and George Fazio and he would have to face another grueling 18 holes in the play-off after looking played-out at the end of the regulation 72. No sensible person would have dared to bet a dime against him, knowing the character of a man able to pick himself up from such devastating circumstances, but the odds were surely stacked against him. Hogan not only won—he did so with a 69 to Mangrum's 73 and Fazio's 75.

This win provided the perfect recuperative medicine, injecting new life into Hogan's accident-battered frame. It seemed as though fate had rewarded a man's fight back against dire odds. Hogan was to win the U.S. Masters and the U.S. Open in 1951 and he repeated that double achievement in 1953. Next on the menu in 1953 for the galloping golfer was a taste of the British Open on the sun-baked links of Carnoustie. Hogan made no bones about his distaste for Carnoustie, with the fairways scarred by divot marks and the greens only improving as the rains came later in the week, but he delivered some tasty golf appreciated by every Scot who saw it.

He mastered the course, and at the age of 40 he won the Open Championship. Benjamin William Hogan, or "Bantam Ben" as some called him, had played in his first and only Open. He had won three majors in one year and he might have completed what would become known as the Grand Slam if the U.S. P.G.A. Championship had not been held at the same time as the Open Championship. It had been a year of exemplary play. Yet Hogan belonged to that rare breed for whom there is always another summit to climb. He was the habitual trier. His comeback from that death-defying crash, and his impressive performances in 1953 probably provided him with a high point on which to retire. But the irrepressible golfer continued. Fate would, however, swing against him for he finished runner-up in the U.S. Masters both in 1954, when he was beaten in a play-off by Sam Snead, and in 1955, and came second in the U.S. Open both in 1955, when he was edged out in a play-off by the virtually unknown Jack Fleck, and in 1956.

Hogan, who had emulated Sarazen by winning each of the four major championships at least once during his career, would make one final run for the U.S. Open in 1960. But now he had become a victim of the putting yips and he also faced competition from a man called Palmer who would revitalize the game on both sides of the Atlantic.

Hogan's decision not to defend the Open Championship at Royal Birkdale in 1954 opened the door to a new champion. This time the up-and-coming kid was an Australian called Peter Thomson. He had turned professional in 1949 and because there were very few tournaments in his native country he came to play mostly in Britain where he charmed the spectators as a disciple of the basic fundamentals of the game. Thomson was to win three years in succession from 1954—the first player to do so since Bob Ferguson in the 1880s—and once more in 1958 when he overcame the Welshman Dave Thomas in a 36-hole play-off at Royal Lytham and St. Annes. Thomas's game was sound from tee to green, but his lack of authority on and around the putting surfaces proved his undoing, and he lost the play-off by four strokes, while Henry Cotton finished six shots behind Thomson and Thomas.

Thomson's spell was only broken in 1957 when at St. Andrews Locke emerged from a state of semi-retirement to win his fourth Open Championship, following triumphs in 1949, 1950, and 1952, by finishing three shots in front of the Australian.

Locke had taken up the mantle following Cotton's last win in 1948—Max Faulkner was to give Britain her last champion for 18 years with his success in 1951—and like Thomson he was happier playing in Europe. He was christened "Muffin Face" in America because of his change-less expression, but it was crossing swords with American officials that really hurt Locke. There is a theory that some Americans were put out when Locke scooped up dollars by winning six times in 1947 on the U.S. Tour, then taking the lucrative Tam o'Shanter in 1950.

Locke nevertheless became a familiar figure in Britain and he and Thomson dominated the 1950s. Locke, skinny as a child, is best remembered striding across the fairways in a most leisurely manner, as if he was out for a walk, and he stood out too in his plus-fours, collar, tie, and the famous white cap. He seemed remarkably serene at times, and his ice-cold putting technique would put the yips in his opponents.

Left: A jaunty-looking Peter Thomson photographed during the Piccadilly World Match Play Championships at Wentworth, England, 1967. Thomson lost in the final to Arnold Palmer.

Right: Byron Nelson (left) and Harry Weetman, captains of the U.S. and Great Britain 1965 Ryder Cup teams respectively, shake hands at Royal Birkdale, Southport, England.

Left: Bobby Locke of South Africa shakes hands with Ireland's Harry Bradshaw. After putting out on the 18th hole at Royal St. George's in 1949 Locke tied with Bradshaw for the Open Championship, but went on to win the play-off, then played over 36-holes.

Above: Welsh golfer Dai Rees in action at the 1952 Daks tournament played at Wentworth a fortnight before the Open Championship.

Right: The view over hole ten at the Royal Lytham and St. Annes Golf Club.

Locke, however, seemed by accident rather than design to become involved in controversy. In 1949, the year of his first Open Championship win, he was to beat Harry Bradshaw of Ireland in a play-off at Royal St. George's. Bradshaw, might have won but for an incident at the fifth hole in the second round. There he found his ball in a broken beer bottle. He could have taken a free drop but he elected to play the ball, even though he might damage his eyes if the glass splintered. As luck would have it, the six that he marked on his card eventually made the difference between winning and losing.

To beat Thomson in 1957, however, Locke had to survive a stewards' enquiry. On the last green Locke was asked by his Australian playing partner Bruce Crampton to mark his ball one clubhead's length away. He did so, some three feet from the hole, but when he replaced it Locke absent-mindedly put it back where his marker now stood. It was an innocent error and the officials decided to take no action.

In the wake of Snead and Hogan, the U.S. produced a succession of fine players. Doug Ford won the U.S. P.G.A. Championship in 1955 and the U.S. Masters two years later. Cary Middlecoff won the U.S. Masters in 1955 and the U.S. Open 12 months later. Jackie Burke completed a memorable double when in 1956 he won the U.S. Masters followed by the U.S. P.G.A. Championship. Then came Arnold Palmer who brought class and charisma to the game.

Golf was soaring toward the sixties, with prize money on the U.S. Tour alone reaching an astonishing $1 million in 1958. The sport was getting more TV coverage—and growing numbers of people were watching the game. With all this interest, some outstanding women players emerged.

Left: The wild landscape of Royal Birkdale Golf Club. This is the second hole.

WOMEN TO THE FORE

Right: The incomparable Laura Davies was still winning titles as the new millennium dawned.

Arnold Palmer was to enrich the game in a manner that no other golfer of his time, or any other era, would emulate. A social revolution was taking place, on as well as off the fairways, and Palmer generated excitement as the traditional tweed look gave way to color co-ordinated outfits. His hitch-the-pants and go-for-broke style suited the swinging sixties. A man of daring deeds, he would become the darling of the fairways, influencing both men and women players.

Mark McCormack, a college chum, would see to it that Palmer's skills would revolutionize the sport. McCormack became Palmer's manager and he would in time become the most powerful entrepreneur in the game, the agent for numerous sportsmen and sportswomen.

There can be no doubt that women have long been prominent in golf. Rosalynde Cossey, one of the leading authorities on the women's game, pinpoints Catherine of Aragon, the first wife of Henry VIII, as the earliest recorded female advocate of the sport. In 1513, while Henry was rampaging in France, Catherine, as governor of the realm, saw off the invading Scots and still had time to note that the game was in good shape: "All his (Henry's) subjects be very glad I thank God to be busy with the Golfe for they take it for pastime; my heart is very good to it."

The Scots undoubtedly lost a few good players at the Battle of Flodden that same year, but half a century and more later Mary Queen of Scots was roundly criticized after being spotted taking a gentle thwack or two "on the playing fields outside Seton" only a couple of days after the dreadful murder of her husband, Lord Darnley. Her reputation never really recovered.

It was another couple of hundred years before women further down the social scale took any real interest in the game but by the late 18th century the fishwives of Musselburgh, strong active people, were noted for their prowess, and they resolutely set about forming themselves into a society at their course near the city of Edinburgh.

In the early 19th century women also played at St. Andrews but were generally frowned upon. And, according to Miss A.M. Stewart, "a damsel with even one modest putter in her hand was labelled a fast and almost disreputable person, definitely one to be avoided."

The female of the species has a stubborn streak, however, and will insist on playing despite the handicaps of dress, decorum, and masculine derision. The St. Andrews Ladies' Golf Club was formed in 1867, the first of its kind anywhere in the world, and the following year the Westward Ho! and North Devon Ladies' Club was founded in the southwest of England. There the only club allowed was a wooden putter, which made the advice of Horace Hutchinson, golfer and writer, seem irrelevant:

"We venture to suggest 70 or 80 yards as the average limit of a drive advisedly; not because we doubt a lady's power to make a longer drive

Top: Catherine of Aragon, first wife of Henry VIII, has been described as the first female advocate of the game.

Above: Mary Queen of Scots was a keen participant in golf although this was eventually to prove a considerable handicap to her. In 1567 she was spotted playing the game at Seton House soon after her husband's death, and that was used as evidence at her trial of her complicity in his demise.

Right: Cecil Leitch, four times winner of the British Women's Amateur Championship, pictured at Sheringham in 1920.

but because that cannot well be done without raising the club above the shoulder. Now we do not presume to dictate, but we must observe that the posture and gestures requisite for a full swing are not particularly graceful when the player is clad in female dress."

One shudders to think what Mr. Hutchinson would make of someone like Laura Davies, who has been known to boom drives of 300 yards and more, delivering a healthy, uninhibited belt to the ball and worrying about the direction later.

Laura's forerunners set up the Ladies' Golf Union in 1893 and held the first British Amateur Championship that same year. It was won by Lady Margaret Scott, whose father had a course laid out in his private park. Thus advantaged, Lady Margaret won the title in 1894 and 1895 as well before retiring from the competitive game.

Over on the other side of the Atlantic the women's game was also beginning to take hold and the first United States Golf Association Women's Amateur Championship was played at the Meadow Brook Club, Hempstead, New York, on November 9, 1895. It was arranged at short notice and featured a mere 13 competitors, playing nine holes before lunch and nine holes after. The winner was Mrs. Charles S. Brown of the Shinnecock Hills Club, with a score of 132–69 for the first nine and 63 for the second.

In 1896 the championship became match-play and Beatrix Hoyt of Shinnecock won the first of her three successive titles. She was aged 16. In 1900, at the tender age of 20, she gave up tournament golf.

The Curtis sisters, Margaret and Harriot, of the Essex Country Club, Manchester, Massachusetts, were a formidable presence in American golf at this time and between them

won the Amateur four times between 1906 and 1912. In 1905, they traveled to Britain for the Ladies' Championship at Cromer in Norfolk and they and the other Americans with them played a match against a side called England but containing several Scottish and Irish players.

"England" won 6-1 and the occasion was such a success that the Curtis sisters were keen to present a cup for future matches. They had their wish but it was not until 1932 that the Curtis Cup was officially instituted, with the United States beating Great Britain and Ireland at Wentworth in England. It was not until 1986 that a British and Irish side managed to win on American soil, overcoming not only their opponents at Prairie Dunes but also the alien conditions of a Kansas summer when temperatures soared to over 100 degrees Fahrenheit. Captained by Diane Bailey, it was the first golf team, male or female, amateur or professional, to succeed in defeating the Americans on their own soil.

Competing in that first Curtis Cup match were Joyce Wethered and Glenna Collett (Mrs. E.H. Vare), two golfers who dominated their contemporaries and were undoubted giants of the game. In the top singles, the last match the two played against each other in major competition,

Above: Joyce Wethered with her trophy when she won the British Women's Amateur Championship in 1929 at St. Andrews.

Far Left: In this advertisement for a silk sports coat the model holds a golf club—a sign of the increasing popularity of the game among women at the turn of the century.

Wethered defeated Vare by six and four, thus confirming her superiority.

In a classic encounter in the final of the British at St. Andrews in 1929, Joyce Wethered recovered from five down after 11 holes to beat Miss Collett (as she then was) at the 35th and win the title for the fourth time. Bobby Jones, who knew a thing or two, described Wethered as the best player, man or woman, that he had ever encountered.

Glenna Collett failed to win a British title, losing in the final twice, but she more than compensated by winning the U.S. Women's Amateur no fewer than six times—a record. She took over from Alexa Stirling, a childhood friend of Jones in Atlanta, Georgia, as America's outstanding woman player. Stirling won her native title three times in a row, in 1916, 1919, and 1920, with the First World War intervening in 1917 and 1918. Then Miss Collett made her debut.

Her forceful robust personality made her a formidable competitor; she won the first of her titles in 1922 and the last, under her married name, in 1935. In more recent times she has given her name to the Vare Trophy, which is awarded annually to the player with the lowest stroke average on the Ladies' Professional Golf Association tour.

Women professionals were thin on the ground in Mrs. Vare's heyday, though in the mid-1930s Miss Wethered did forfeit her amateur status and traveled to America where she played a series of popular exhibition matches with the likes of Gene Sarazen and Babe Zaharias. Miss Wethered became Lady Heathcoat Amory not long afterward and was reinstated as an amateur after the Second World War, by which time she was devoting most of her energies to gardening.

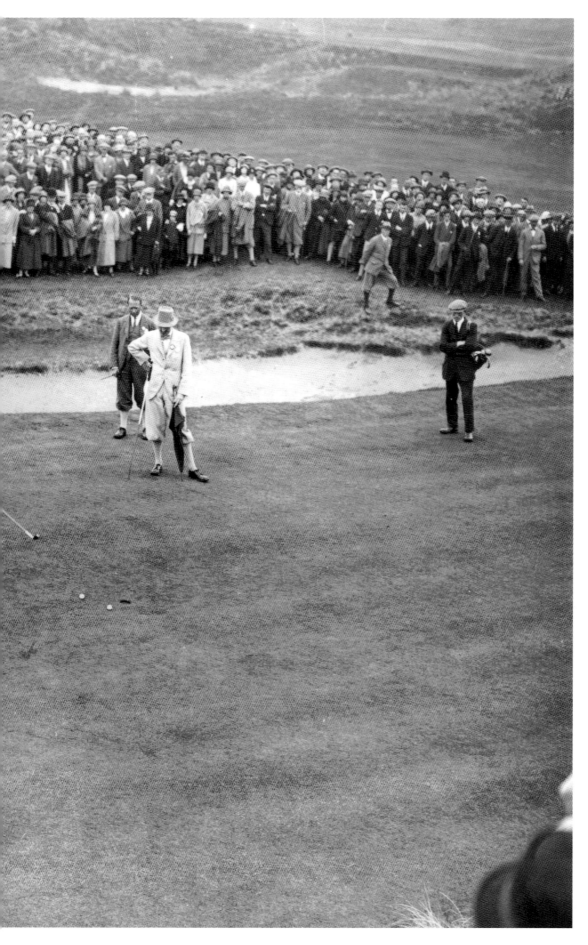

Left: Joyce Wethered in action on the green during the 1925 Ladies' British Open Amateur Championship at Troon. Wethered was considered to be the best female golfer of her time and went on to win the competition in this year for the third time in her career.

"The Babe," who had won two gold medals at the Olympic Games in 1932, was one of the great personalities of women's sport. She turned to golf with relish, establishing a reputation for fearsome hitting, even though she was by no stretch of the imagination a large woman. "I just hitch up my girdle and let it rip," she revealed when asked for the secret.

In 1935 she won the Texas Open and was then banned from playing in amateur events, only being reinstated in 1943. That opened the way for her to win the U.S. Amateur in 1946 and the British title the following year, the first American to do so. She stunned the crowds at Gullane, near Edinburgh, not only with her golf but with her extroverted behavior. On the day of the final she appeared in red and white checked shorts which she was asked, firmly, to go back and change.

The Babe turned professional for good after that and picked up her first U.S. Women's Open title in 1948, the year the Women's Professional Golf Association, founded four years earlier, foundered. "It didn't collapse financially," said Betty Hicks, a prime mover behind it, "it just sort of faded away."

In 1950 the W.P.G.A.'s replacement, the Ladies' Professional Golf Association, was fully fledged and as it flourished so prize money increased from $50,000 to the extent that more than $37 million was at stake in more than 40 events in 2000 when Ty M. Votaw, the sixth commissioner of the L.P.G.A., began his first full year at the helm having begun his tenure on March 24, 1999. The pioneers were people like Betty Jameson, the first glamour girl of the tour, Marlene Hagge, Alice Bauer, Bettye Danoff, Shirley Spork, Helen Dettweiler, Helen Hicks, Opal Hill,

Left: The Great Britain and Ireland team, which drew 4½-4½ in the Curtis Cup match with the United States at Gleneagles, Scotland in 1936, are (left to right): Miss P. Wade, Miss Pam Barton, Mrs. A. Holm, Miss B. Newell, Mrs. J.B. Walker, Miss J. Anderson. Seated: Mrs. P. Jaron, Miss D.E. Chambers (captain) and Miss Wanda Morgan.

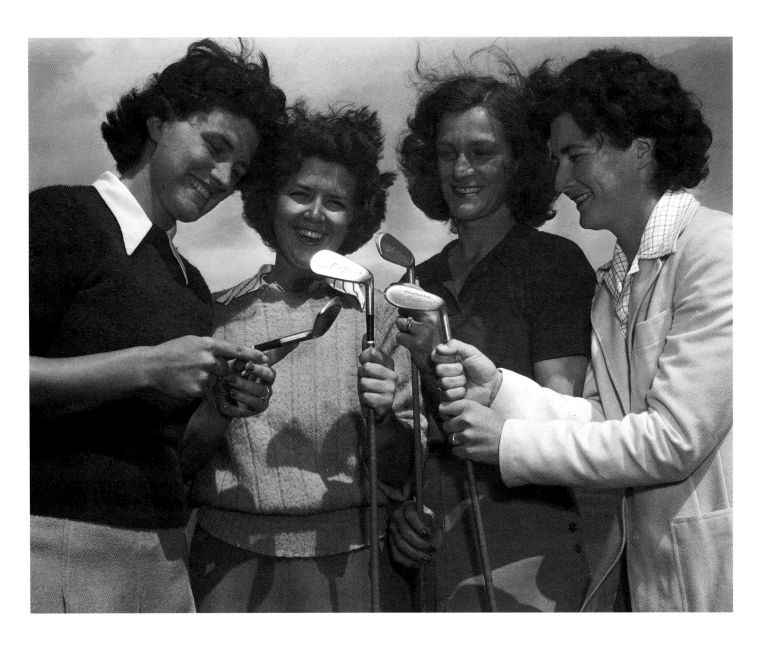

Above: Examining their clubs are (left to right) Dot Germain, Phyllis Otto, "Babe" Zaharias, and Louise Suggs. Each had just won their second round matches and entered the quarter finals of the 1945, 45th Annual Amateur Tournament of the Women's Western Golf association.

Sally Sessions, Louise Suggs, Patty Berg, Marilynn Smith, and Babe Zaharias, all founder members of the L.P.G.A., and others such as Peggy Kirk and Betsy Rawls to mention but two.

The U.S. Women's Open Championship was instituted in 1946 and was won by Miss Berg, who beat Miss Jameson by five and four in the final at the Spokane Country Club. The format was changed to stroke-play the next year and Miss Jameson won with 295, the first time, as far as anyone can ascertain, that 300 was bettered in a women's 72-hole tournament.

After that came the Babe who was runner-up in 1949, albeit a comprehensive 14 shots behind Miss Suggs. Her second title came in 1950, but it is her third victory that is most remembered, for it took place in 1954, a year after she had undergone surgery for cancer. At the Salem Country Club in Peabody, Massachusetts, her total of 291 was only three over par and left her 12 shots clear of the runner-up, Miss Hicks. The Babe never defended her title and died aged just 42 in September 1956.

Her successor as the dominant figure on the tour, in playing terms at least, was Mickey Wright (born Mary Kathryn), a quiet, retiring woman

who would deserve her place among the golfing greats. She turned professional in 1956 and gave due warning of what was to come by winning her first tournament, the Jacksonville Open. Over the next 13 years she was to win 81 events, including an unprecedented 13 major titles, and added an 82nd in 1973, four years after she had stopped playing regularly on the Tour. Only Kathy Whitworth has won more tournaments—88 in all—but she would defer to Miss Wright in terms of ability and sheer class.

Wright's accomplishments are legend and if she had been a more flamboyant personality, with even a touch of "the Babe's" talent for publicity, she would certainly be better known as one of the superstars of the game. As a rule Mickey Wright let her golf do the talking—though she did become the first player to be fined by the L.P.G.A. when she criticized the round-robin format of an event she failed to win, despite the fact that her scoring had been generally superior to that of the opposition.

Miss Wright won four U.S. Open titles—a record shared by Betsy Rawls—four L.P.G.A. Championships, three Western Opens, and two Titleholders' Championships, all components of

Above: Patty Berg in action in 1936. She went on to win the U.S. Amateur Championship in 1938 and a total of 40 tournaments as an amateur before turning professional. She was the first woman to reach $100,000 in career winnings and she won no fewer than 80 tournaments as a professional.

the women's Grand Slam. She won three of the four majors on offer in 1961, a feat that was not matched until Pat Bradley, having her year of years, won a total of three out of four in 1986.

Miss Wright was one of the greatest streak players the game has ever known. Once she was in the groove she could win and win and win again. In 1961 it was ten tournaments; in 1962 it was ten again, including four in a row; in 1963 she won four in a row again, amassing 13 in all; in 1964 she relented slightly and won only 11. In that four-year period, she came second 19 times and, hardly surprisingly, she admitted she felt invincible.

"It got to the point," she said, "where my swing was good enough that I felt I could not shoot a bad round. It was a feeling that stayed with me for four years."

Right: Nancy Lopez chips the ball to the 16th green during the first round of the Colgate European Women's Championship at Sunningdale. Lopez became the darling of America's fairways during the 1980s.

The trouble with that sort of dominance is that the moment you fail to win everyone clamors to know why. "That gets to be more than you can handle," reflected Miss Wright, who eventually suffered from what she described as "emotional fatigue" because she was in contention week in, week out. "It finally just wore me out," she said. She was only in her mid-thirties when she stopped competing regularly and the L.P.G.A. player guide cites a variety of reasons including "reaction to sunlight, aversion to flying, and foot problems."

A few years later in the mid-1970s the Tour itself was having problems. Prize money had risen to over $1 million, but the L.P.G.A. was having trouble coping with its rapid expansion and was on the verge of bankruptcy. In 1975, Ray Volpe was appointed as the first Commissioner of the L.P.G.A. and set about sorting things out. So successful was he that in his seven years with the Association prize money alone soared from $1.5 million to nearly $6.5 million.

Volpe's promotion of the women's Tour was given the boost it needed with the arrival of that rare, unpredictable, magical being—a superstar. Not just a good player but a good player who was delightful, charming, immensely attractive, and full of life. Nancy Lopez had arrived, and the Tour had lift-off.

The public took to Nancy and her smile immediately and in her first full season on the Tour she won nine tournaments, including five in a row, eclipsing the feats of Mickey Wright and Kathy Whitworth, both of whom had won four. Television cameras recorded her every move while Miss Lopez was in Rochester, New York, for the aptly named Bankers Trust Classic, the tournament that would give her the record. She

did not disappoint, coming from three shots behind with a round to play, to win by two.

Her play may have impressed the fans—and they flocked to watch her—but it was her composure that impressed her fellow professionals. JoAnne Carner, no mean performer herself, with five U.S. Amateur titles to her name and two U.S. Opens, not to mention hordes of other honors, said of Nancy's performance, "Nancy handled the pressure unbelievably. In fact, she seemed to thrive on it. For someone that young [Lopez was 21] not to be overwhelmed was the most amazing thing."

Lopez proved her success was no fluke by winning eight tournaments the following year and topping the money list again. She was number one for the third time in 1985, winning a mere five times but silencing most of the critics who had said she would not last. Her swing, highly individualistic, contained at least ten faults, they said, and could not possibly stand the strain of a career on the Tour.

In 1987, having taken most of the previous year off to have her second child, Nancy Lopez (by this time happily married to baseball star Ray Knight after an unsuccessful first marriage) won the second tournament of the season, the Sarasota Classic, to earn herself a place in the Hall of Fame, alongside the likes of Berg, Zaharias, Wright, and Carner. It is an exclusive club, with only 17 player members and one honorary at the turn of the new millennium, and Miss Lopez was inducted with due pomp and ceremony in the glittering setting of Tiffany's on Fifth Avenue.

If there is one glaring gap in Miss Lopez's record it is that she has not won the U.S. Women's Open. This is not an omission that

figures in the career of Laura Davies, the tall, blonde, English woman. Indeed Davies's first success on American soil came in the U.S. Women's Open. Davies was more or less unheralded when she arrived in Plainfield, New Jersey, for the 1987 Open, though a few people knew of her reputation for long hitting.

By the end of the extended championship—it lasted six days because of a thunderstorm and a play-off—she had become a celebrity and won

Far Left: Nancy Lopez was a constant winner despite the fact that critics found at least ten faults with her highly individualistic swing.

Far Left Below: Julie Inkster won the American Ladies' Amateur Championship three years in succession, from 1980 to 1982. She later made a successful transition from amateur to professional.

Left: Laura Davies won the Ladies British Open in 1986, and finished runner-up in 1987 when she captured the U.S. Women's Open title.

Right: Ayako Okamoto became in 1982 only the second Japanese golfer to win on the United States L.P.G.A. circuit when she won the Arizona Copper Classic.

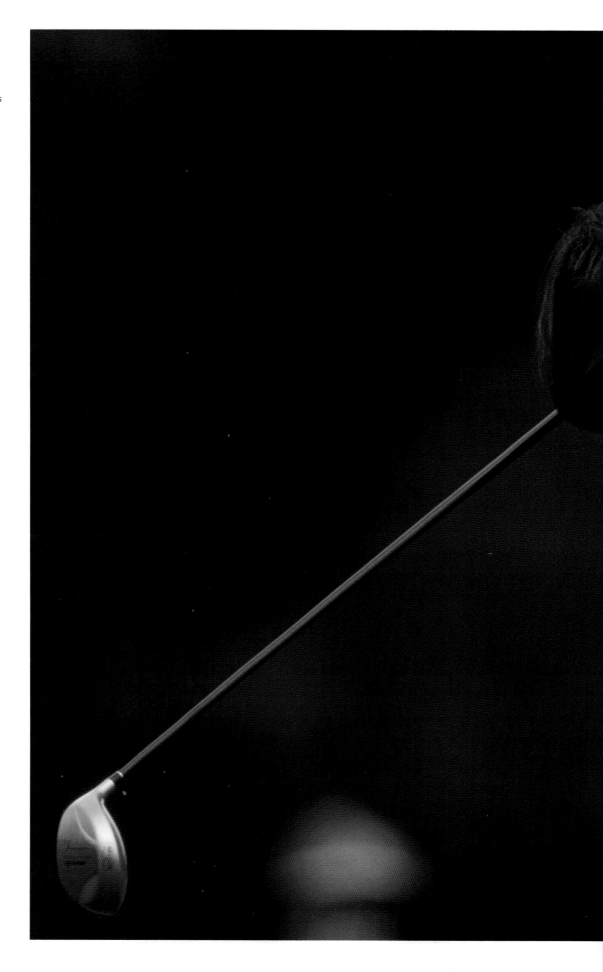

the title. She defeated JoAnne Carner as well as Ayako Okamoto of Japan (who all season had been vying with Betsy King and Jane Geddes at the top of the money list) in an 18-hole play-off, leaving them slightly bemused by her enormous power and immense calm—and mightily impressed by her talent.

Miss Davies's intention had been to attend the L.P.G.A.'s qualifying events in a bid to earn her card for 1988 but the Association had the good sense to change its rules and exempt her from qualifying. Any non-L.P.G.A. member who won one of the tour's domestic events would be eligible to compete the following season without the formality of qualifying. The situation had not arisen before because of the three previous foreign winners of the Open, Fay Crocker, a Uruguayan, was an L.P.G.A. member, as was Jan Stephenson, the glamorous Australian, and the remarkable Catherine Lacoste of France was an amateur.

Miss Lacoste was 22 years and five days old when she won the title in 1967 and remains the only amateur winner. Two years later, she won both the British Amateur and the U.S. Amateur titles, following Dorothy Campbell (1909) and Pam Barton (1936) as the third person to achieve that particular double.

The day of the great amateur would die with the advent of professional golf. Clearly the rewards have become so great that there is no incentive for the budding Bobby Joneses to remain attached to the amateur ranks. That is not a criticism, rather a statement of fact, and the world of golf would most certainly be emptier without some of the outstanding amateurs who have graced the fairways over the years.

Nobody, for instance, will ever equal the achievement of John Ball in winning the British Amateur no fewer than eight times, the last occasion being at Westward Ho! with his success in 1912. Ball's brilliant performances took place before Americans began to compete regularly in the Amateur Championship with the inauguration of the Walker Cup.

That match began on the eve of the Amateur Championship at Royal Liverpool in 1921, although the first official encounter between Great Britain and Ireland and the United States did not take place until the following year. It came about after a rules meeting between the Royal and Ancient and the United States Golf Association at which George Herbert Walker of the National Links of America was present in his capacity as the President of the U.S.G.A. Walker, fired by the suggestion of a regular fixture between the nations, offered a trophy, and with a little assistance from various newspapers the match became known as the Walker Cup.

Initially the tournament was played annually but like the Ryder Cup, the professional counterpart, it subsequently became a biennial affair following the 1924 contest during which it was pointed out that a meeting every other year might help the longevity of the match.

When the teams did meet again in 1926, with Bobby Jones beating Cyril Tolley 12 and 11 as the Americans squeezed to a narrow win, it was clear that the golfers from the United States were establishing a supremacy in a sport initially popularized by the British nation. Jess Sweetner, for instance, was to win the Amateur Championship in 1926 and so start a trend, with Americans winning consistently in Walker Cup

Left: Charles Coe, the captain, and his teammate Harvie Ward, hold the Walker Cup once again following America's victory at Muirfield in 1959.

years in Britain right up until 1963 when Michael Lunt broke the spell.

It is the U.S. Amateur Championship of 1930, however, which lives longest in the memory of golfing historians. For it was that year at Merion that the Grand Slam dream of Bobby Jones came to fruition as he beat Eugene Homans eight and seven to complete his unprecedented four-timer. Jones had won the British and U.S. Opens and the British and U.S. Amateur Championships. The U.S. Amateur in 1930 was to be his last championship.

Even so, 12 months later the U.S. Amateur was again to become headline news. What could one say as Francis Ouimet, the hero of the 1913 U.S. Open, followed Jones by winning the 1931 U.S. Amateur title—17 years after his first win in 1914. The irony is that Jack Westland, whom Ouimet defeated in that final, was himself to

Right: Bobby Jones driving from the fairway during the 1930 Open Championship.

create a record in 1952 by winning the championship at the age of 48 to become the oldest champion at that time.

As time progressed so the U.S. Amateur champions led by the likes of Arnold Palmer and Jack Nicklaus, the winners in 1954 and 1959 respectively, would become familiar names in the professional world. Palmer, however, turned professional shortly afterward whereas Nicklaus waited until 1961 when he overcame Dudley Wysong eight and six in the final to win again at Pebble Beach.

It was not until the 1970s, however, that the U.S. Amateur champions became recognized for making a successful transition to the professional ranks. Lanny Wadkins (1970), Craig Stadler (1973), Jerry Pate (1974), John Cook (1978), Mark O'Meara (1979), and Hal Sutton (1980) were to change the trend and, later, Phil Mickelson, Justin Leonard, and Tiger Woods

would emphasis the point. The same, perhaps, cannot be said of the British Amateur, except perhaps for the success of José Maria Olazábal of Spain in 1984, and the emergence, more recently, of his compatriot, Sergio Garcia, who won the Amateur at Muirfield in 1998.

Olazábal's star moved into ascendancy with that sparkling triumph and it also illuminated the increasing influence that players from the continent of Europe would have on the game of golf. That influence has shown itself in the Ryder Cup, with the inclusion of continental players and victories over the United States, but in the Walker Cup there remains a strictly Great Britain and Ireland team. The Americans, as in the Ryder Cup, dominated the early years of this biennial match but the the British and Irish team, who won for the first time on American soil in 1989 at Peachtree, Atlanta, now has five victories to its credit following successes in 1995 at Royal

Left: Jerry Pate, the US Amateur champion in 1974, successfully switched to the pro ranks and won the U.S.Open in 1976.

Right: Hal Sutton was another U.S. amateur champion who made a smooth switch to the professionals, and in the year 2000 he won his 12th U.S. Tour event when he captured The Players Championship.

Porthcawl in Wales and 1999 at Nairn in Scotland.

The emergence of Tiger Woods, with successive U.S. Amateur Championship wins in 1994, 1995, and 1996, provided food for thought for others coming into the game, although looking back it is difficult to imagine in the 21st century any player ever again dominating amateur golf as did Bobby Jones and, for that matter, Michael Bonallack. Peter McEvoy, who captained the winning Great Britain and Ireland Walker Cup team in 1999, won the Amateur Championship twice, but Bonallack gained no fewer than five victories during his illustrious career. He became secretary to the Royal and Ancient, retiring in 1999, and nowadays it would be most unlikely for any golfer with raw talent to remain amateur.

The attraction of turning professional for women golfers became increasingly evident towards the end of the 20th century with the growth of the L.P.G.A. and the Ladies European Tour. The emergence of a number of great champions from a whole host of nations was, unquestionably significant, with Karrie Webb from Australia and Se Ri Pak from South Korea challenging the likes of Sweden's Annika Sorenstam, Britain's Laura Davies, Canada's Lorie Kane, and Americans such as Juli Inkster, Meg Mallon, and Dottie Pepper.

The 1990s had seen the introduction of the Solheim Cup, the first Ryder Cup-type event for professional women golfers, and if this further helped popularize the women's game so did the international leaderboards at the top events. Webb, from Queensland, had already won the Weetabix Women's British Open (1995) before she enjoyed at the age of 21 a phenomenal rookie season in America in 1996. She became the first rookie golfer in history—man or women—to reach the $1 million mark in single-season earnings. She was number one on the L.P.G.A. Tour that year and again in 1999 with a record $1.591 million then began the new millennium by winning the first event of 2000. By then many

observers were insisting that Webb had become to the L.P.G.A. what Woods was on the P.G.A. Tour—the dominant golfer.

All of which provided the women's game with much to celebrate and especially the L.P.G.A., as for them the new millennium, coincidentally, kicked off their 50th anniversary celebrations. The founder members in 1950 had totaled 13 in all. They were strong-willed, competitive women, but although they triggered an explosion in popularity for the women's game, and fought on the front lines to legitimize the concept of women as athletes, even the likes of Suggs, who was there as the anniversary celebrations began, must still be amazed at what

their so-called "labor of love" achieved. The benefactors, of course, included Karrie Webb and also Se Ri Pak, the Rookie of the Year on the L.P.G.A. Tour in 1998. Pak had finished third behind Webb and the American Julie Inkster on the 1999 L.P.G.A. money list.

Aged 22 when the new millennium dawned, both Pak and Webb were well positioned, brimming with confidence, and enjoying the riches of the 21st century game. Even so, they were still well aware of the enormous rivalry that existed between such as Inkster and Sorenstam, Mallon and Davies, eager to remain at the top of a game they had most certainly helped reach new heights.

Above: Juli Inkster (right) hugs Meg Mallon after winning at the 1999 McDonalds L.P.G.A. Championship.

Left: British golfer Michael Bonallack during his playing days when he was five-times British Amateur Champion. During the year that this photograph was taken (1971) he captained the Walker Cup Team and was awarded the O.B.E. In 1998 he received a knighthood for his services to golf as both a competitor and administrator.

Right: JoAnne Carner, recognized as one of the longest hitters in the game, at the 1993 L.P.G.A. Championships in Bethesda, Maryland.

Inkster was a case in point. The Californian had turned professional in 1983, but in 1999 she enjoyed her finest year—winning five times, including two major championships, and earning $1.337 million to be second on the money list. She thoroughly enjoyed, like Amy Alcott and Beth Daniel with 29 and 32 career wins respectively, gaining entrance to the L.P.G.A. Hall of Fame as they all did in 1999. Inkster won the U.S. Women's Open and McDonald's L.P.G.A. Championship to become only the second women in L.P.G.A. history after Pat Bradley in

1986 to complete the modern day Grand Slam. It seemed it was in her nature to rip open the record book as she had in 1980, 1981, and 1982 to become the first women since 1934 to win three consecutive U.S. Amateur titles.

What it also confirmed was that even as Webb and Woods prepared to launch their attempts to dominate the game in the first decade of the new millennium so there would always be another challenger around the corner as the mighty Arnold Palmer had discovered some 40 years earlier.

Left: A jubilant Betsy King holds the U.S. Women's Open trophy for cameras in 1989 after winning by four shots from Nancy Lopez at Indianwood Golf Club, Lake Orion, Michigan.

THE BIG THREE

Right: Arnold Palmer, who along with Jack Nicklaus and Gary Player, formed the "Big Three" that dominated world golf during the 1960s.

Arnold Palmer broke the ice when he won the U.S. Masters in 1958. Then along came Gary Player and Jack Nicklaus. These three players, together referred to as the "Big Three," would dominate the golf scene in vastly contrasting manner, although there is no doubt whatsoever that Palmer was responsible for changing the game's image.

Palmer had grown up on a golf course. His father, M.J. (Deke) Palmer was employed by a steel and electric company in Latrobe, Pennsylvania, and he became manager of a nine-hole course built there in 1921 some eight years before Arnold was born. Deke made extra money teaching during the depression years and Arnold was born at a time when golf professionals were not expected to set foot in clubhouses.

The story goes that Arnold started his multi-million-pound empire at the age of nine. He had already learned the fundamentals of the game by spending much of his time with his father. He began using that experience to help women members at the club who struggled to hit their shots across the stream that cut the fourth fairway. He took their shots—for a few cents, of course!

Palmer, then, had the ability from a tender age not only to play the game but to sell his talent, and this unique combination of golfing skills and business acumen would pay handsome dividends throughout his career. Golfaholic Palmer benefited enormously from being guided by Mark McCormack the workaholic, but McCormack is the first to point out the reasons behind Palmer's astonishing business success. In his book *The Wonderful World of Professional Golf* McCormack writes about Palmer:

"If you watch Palmer long enough with corporate executives you begin to appreciate why he gets along so well with them. Right or wrong, like it or not, a lot of high-level American business is conducted on the fairways and in the grill rooms of the country clubs.

"The atmosphere is at once congenial, exclusive, and fraternal. There is a universal challenge: the game. It puts everyone on common ground, and humbles all. The man it humbles least is a welcome and worthy inspiration in such circles. I wonder what value can be put on the phrase: 'As Arnold Palmer explained to me just the other day…' That is the currency of VIP golf. Palmer understands this. He maintains his role as star. Yet as he sits there in his cashmere with a company president and the chairman of a board, he knows he has his private jet waiting for him, just as they do. He is very much part of their world, and almost regally aware of it."

Others, too, were to become aware of the importance of the business development of the game. Initially, however, Palmer had to prove himself on the fairways. He did so from 1958 to 1964 during which time he won the U.S. Masters four times, the Open Championship twice, and the U.S. Open once.

Right: Mark McCormack linked with Arnold Palmer to form a formidable manager-player partnership.

Below Right: Australian Kel Nagle, seen here playing in the 1960 Open Championship.

Palmer, however, did much more than simply win championships. In 1960 it was his little piece of ideology that revitalized the Open Championship and gave birth to the return of the expression "Grand Slam" for the first time since the great days of Bobby Jones. Palmer had won both the U.S. Masters and the U.S. Open in 1960 and he announced before setting out for the centenary Open Championship at St. Andrews that he was making a bid to win both that Championship and the U.S. P.G.A. Championship. He claimed this was the modern day Grand Slam.

Palmer's idea won through, but he lost. He did not win the Open Championship that year, losing to the Australian Kel Nagle, and he never did win the U.S. P.G.A. Championship. It looked as if he might in 1960 after starting out with a 67, but in the end Jay Hebert emerged as the winner at the Firestone Country Club in Akron, Ohio.

Even so he became immensely popular on the fairways on both sides of the Atlantic. With his cavalier outlook he captured the public's imagination. He was the archetypal hero because even long-handicapped golfers could relate to his power-packed play.

The Palmer view was to go for broke—as he showed when he followed his first Open appearance in 1960 by returning to compete at Royal Birkdale in 1961. This time Palmer won, demonstrating his swashbuckling style with a stroke of such strength and skill that a plaque was placed to mark the spot.

Such accolades are not awarded lightly. The legendary Bobby Jones was given one at Royal Lytham and St. Annes in 1926 after producing a shot at the 17th hole in the final round that is a part of the game's folklore. He was bunkered and his compatriot and rival for the title, Al Watrous, had negotiated the hole in two sound blows so that his ball was already safely on the putting surface. Jones stepped into the sand, facing a shot of some 170 yards, and with his mashie—a five iron—he clipped the ball over the scrubland and onto the green. Watrous, shellshocked by this supreme stroke, three putted and Jones won the title. A plaque was later erected close to the point at which Jones executed his memorable shot. It simply says "R.T. JONES JNR.—The Open Championship—25th June, 1926."

Palmer gained similar immortality farther along the Lancashire coast with a great recovery also in the last round. It came at the 15th hole (which is now the 16th), where the powerful American had leaked his drive slightly too far to the right. The ball buried itself in heavy rough. Most golfers would have satisfied themselves with a recovery from there with a wedge. Palmer took a six iron from his bag and, with a tremendous swish, he hammered the ball some 140 yards so that it came to rest an astonishing 15 feet from the hole. It was a high risk shot because he could have left the ball buried deeper in the rough.

Speaking later Palmer said, "The rough was very deep. My only thought was to get the club through as hard as I could and maybe the ball would run onto the green. I closed the face slightly to get it through as fast as possible and I was amazed that I was able to get it through as fast as I did."

That, then, was the Palmer who captivated the British public, triggering an explosion of interest in the Open Championship, and he won again at Royal Troon in 1962. Palmer had not been present in 1959 at the Open Championship; there another golfer, later to become a cult figure

in his own right, took the title at Muirfield. He was Gary Player and that first major victory for the South African did not come easily. In fact he would shed tears before being crowned the champion.

In a typical rally that would become a trademark of his game, Player came from eight shots behind on the closing day—when 36 holes were played—to win. Yet he took six at the last and as he left the green Player buried his head in his

Above: Arnold Palmer earned plenty of money on the fairways. One of his most highly paid matches was with Bob Hope in the film *Call Me Bwana*. Bob Hope's club is probably the oddest Palmer has ever seen.

IN MEMORIAM

ROBERT TYRE JONES, JR.
MARCH 17, 1902 — DECEMBER 18, 1971

CO-FOUNDER AND PRESIDENT OF
AUGUSTA NATIONAL GOLF CLUB
AND
MASTERS TOURNAMENT

A GENTLEMAN IN EVERY SENSE OF THE WORD
WHOSE LEGENDARY FEATS AS A GOLFER
WILL INSPIRE THOSE WHO PLAY THE GAME
IN ALL THE YEARS TO COME

PRESENTED IN HONOR OF ROBERT TYRE JONES, JR.
BY THE MEMBERS OF AUGUSTA NATIONAL GOLF CLUB
ON THIS 18TH DAY OF MARCH, 1978

Far Left: a determined Arnold Palmer smashes his second shot toward the par-five ninth green during the second round of the Kemper Open, June 2, 1978.

Left: Bobby Jones memorial.

Previous Page: Arnold Palmer gauges the green.

hands in the belief that he had thrown away his chance. His wife Vivienne stood by his side, whispering words of comfort, and it must have seemed an age before Player could smile once more. He had won by two strokes from Fred Bullock and Belgium's Flory van Donck.

Like the Australian Peter Thomson, whom he had succeeded as Open champion, Gary Player was an extremely dedicated man. He had turned professional at the age of 18, intent on following in the footsteps of his illustrious compatriot Bobby Locke, and he did so with a few words of

Above: Intense concentration shows on the face of the legendary Arnold Palmer as he plays from a bunker.

encouragement from Bobby Jones. When Player won the South African Open in 1956 his father wrote to Jones eulogizing the golfing talent of his son. Mr. Player, however, was compelled to report that he could not afford to pay for his son to go to the United States but that if an invitation to the U.S. Masters was received then he would pass the hat among his friends to see if they could obtain the necessary funds. The reply from Jones in August to Player in Johannesburg read simply "Pass the Hat."

This, then, was how Player made his debut in the 1956 U.S. Masters, but it was at Augusta in 1961 that he was to have his first head-to-head duel with Palmer. Player won, with the assistance of a par at the last where he salvaged his four from a bunker, although the tournament is probably best remembered as the one in which Palmer snatched defeat from the jaws of victory.

He came to the 18th hole needing only a par to beat Player. Instead he took six and he didn't even make it into a play-off. Palmer was in a greenside trap in two. He skulled the ball over the green, pitched back to eight feet and two putted. "That is something I thought only happened to other people," groaned Palmer.

Player, however, had won the first of his three U.S. Masters. He was also to win the U.S. Open once—in 1965—and the U.S. P.G.A. Championship twice, and he would also collect the Open Championship again in 1968 at Carnoustie and in 1974 at Royal Lytham and St. Annes. This is a truly remarkable record of a very remarkable man. Because of his attire—he often dressed in an all-black outfit—Player was referred to as the "Man in Black." But that is less than skin deep. Gary Player is Mr. Determination, a golfer with great commitment and a very positive thinker. When

first starting out he never seemed a sure bet, and there is little about him that is orthodox. A fitness freak and food fanatic—he could be caught doing press-ups or eating dried fruit—he obtained the right rewards even if at times he was controversial and outspoken. He has won more than 140 tournaments around the world and when one considers the daunting thousands of miles he has traveled from his South African home to many different venues worldwide his achievements probably match those of any other individual in the history of the game.

Yet when Player, the first overseas golfer to win the U.S. Masters, challenged Palmer, there emerged the one man whose record would, rightly, go down in the history books as the greatest of any golfer. For if ever a word were coined in the English language to describe a giant of legendary stature it would fit Jack William Nicklaus to a tee in his role as a golfer.

So much has been said and written of Nicklaus and his awesome ability as a competitor that further words seem superfluous. He is without doubt regarded by most followers of the

Above Left: South African Gary Player at the 1956 Daks Tournament in Wentworth.

Above: Jack Nicklaus and Gary Player in discussion.

Left: Gary Player in 1964 at the
World Match-Play Championship
playing with Arnold Palmer.

Right: Gary Player photographed at the 1999 Senior British Open at Royal Portrush Golf Club in Northern Ireland, where Christy O'Connor Jnr triumphed.

Far Right: Jack Nicklaus (left) shares a joke with Arnold Palmer at the 1987 U.S. Masters.

game as the greatest golfer ever. A statement as emphatic as this is not intended in any way to decry the achievements of such master golfers as Jones or Hagen, Palmer or Player. It is just that every now and then someone of the very highest caliber becomes a yardstick for measuring the achievements of others.

If everyone were to vote for the best golfer ever then the likes of Jones, Hogan, Palmer, Sarazen, Player, and Tom Watson would all figure in the debate with, perhaps, Seve Ballesteros and Nick Faldo having their supporters, and Tiger Woods now compiling a record which will strengthen his claims. We should not forget the likes of Harry Vardon, but the completed record books of the 20th century surely placed Nicklaus on top of all others. He has to be seen as the number one golfer of all time.

Almost without doubt he could have equaled Bobby Jones's Grand Slam had he elected to remain an amateur. If evidence is needed then one has only to recall the events that unfolded in the U.S. Open at Cherry Hills, Denver, Colorado, in 1960. Mike Souchak led after three rounds on 208, but this most distinguished of fields included Nicklaus, still an amateur, and Ben Hogan, both on 211, Player on 213, Sam Snead on 214, and Palmer

on 215. Nicklaus holed from 20 feet at the short 12th for a birdie two and at that point, with six holes remaining, he led. But as Hogan's hopes sank in the water at the 17th so Palmer continued a charge that would take him past Nicklaus. In fact he overtook no fewer than 14 players that famous last day, coming from seven shots off the pace. It has been correctly stated that a huge slice of the Palmer legend was born

Above: Gary Player demonstrates that he has lost none of his skill over the years at Royal Portrush in 1999.

that day but also the American public realized that in Nicklaus they possessed another great golfer.

Not that they took to Nicklaus easily. Indeed he virtually became public enemy number one two years later at Oakmont Country Club in Palmer's state of Pennsylvania. His crime was to take on, and beat, Palmer in front of a record crowd of 62,000, many of whom formed the swarm of spectators who became known as "Arnie's Army." Nicklaus had won the U.S. Amateur title the previous September and had then decided it was time to turn professional. At Oakmont, however, the pro-Palmer gallery regarded Nicklaus as an intruder. Palmer, raised only 40 miles away, was supposed to win and complete a triumphant return to the Pennsylvania heartland.

Arnie's Army, enlarged this time by a full brigade of iron and steel workers from

Left: Arnold Palmer marks his card at the 1993 Senior British Open at Royal Lytham and St. Annes.

Right: Arnold Palmer salutes the
cameras with his cap at the 1995
Open Championship at St. Andrews.

Pittsburgh, did their level best to destroy Nicklaus. Yet he fought his way into a play-off with Palmer. It was a supreme achievement as Nicklaus, then a rather overweight, crew-cut athlete, had to endure jibe after jibe. "Hey fatty," shouted some members of the gallery. "Hit the ball in here." Those spectators were standing in the rough. Others yelled "Hey, Crisco fat in the can." (Crisco was a packaged cooking product.) And from another section of the crowd came the serious demands of "Step on his ball, Arnie. Kick the thing into the rough."

This, of course, was not what Palmer wanted. As the play-off unfolded he genuinely pleaded with the fans to behave. The helmeted stewards struggled to keep order. Tempers rose beyond boiling point as Nicklaus began to take the initiative. Some reports suggest that beer cans were thrown and that some reporters, there to cover this great head-to-head duel, were pushed into sand bunkers. Nicklaus, however, did not seem to notice the commotion. His blinkered

approach took him to a 71 and Palmer, clearly distracted, shot 74. Jack Nicklaus had arrived and the world of golf now had the Big Three of Palmer, Player, and Nicklaus.

Born in Columbus, Ohio in 1940 Nicklaus was playing golf at the age of ten. He was encouraged by his father Charles, and coached by Jack Grout. At the age of 12 he was breaking 80 and at 16 he was the Ohio State champion. In 1959 came his first U.S. Amateur win after a keen tussle with Charles Coe.

So his career had followed a fairly comfortable path. Now the so-called "fat boy" from the Buckeye State would have to win the spectators to his side. Not that it seemed to bother him as he showed at Oakmont. He clearly understood the love that existed for Palmer and he knew there was one sure way to win the hearts of the supporters: He had to become the best golfer in the world.

Nicklaus had chosen a good time. Palmer's deeds had excited millions and encouraged a

boom in the game. To understand the part that Nicklaus initially played it is important to realize that in America the emotions of the spectators move in highly mysterious but predictable ways. It is good to have a villain playing opposite the hero and in Nicklaus the American public had a perfectly cast villain. What right did this pudgy upstart from Columbus have to beat their flesh and blood superstar?

The evidence of the changes afoot in world golf can be illustrated by the fact that in 1963, for the first time in the history of the U.S. Tour, the leading money winner achieved six figures. The man at the top was Palmer with earnings of $128,230. Golf was becoming an attractive alternative for college kids who more and more took to the fairways rather than to football or baseball fields. So strong was the competition among would-be golfers that the U.S. P.G.A. elected in 1965 to launch a qualifying school for the Tour.

Around the world knowledge of the game was spreading, with countries such as Greece and Israel laying out their first courses in the early 1960s. But nowhere was the growth of the game accelerating as rapidly as it was in the United States. There the game grew at such a rate that by 1968 the tournament players had separated

Above: Tony Lema's winning performance at the Open Championship in 1964, which was played on the Old Course, St. Andrews.

Right: Jack Nicklaus with the coveted silver claret jug of the Open Championship. He had his first such win in 1966—at his fifth attempt—and went on to win it a further two times in 1970 and 1978.

from the P.G.A. to form their own body. Joe Dey was the first commissioner and prize money began to rocket. The U.S. Tour had been worth $150,000 in 1938. By 1952 the figure was $500,000, then by 1973 $8 million. In 1990 the U.S. Tour played for $46 million and for the millennium season Tom Finchem, now the Commissioner, announced that "the new century will feature a record 49 official events. Along with more playing opportunities, our members will compete for approximately $157 million in official prize money, up from $135 million in 1999."

The growth of the game, of course, had been sparked by the Palmer era and he continued to

Left: Jack Nicklaus on his way to a famous comeback triumph at the U.S. Masters in Augusta, 1986.

play a leading role in the promotion of the game as the 1960s and 1970s unfolded. However, he ceased to be a force in the major championships. Player would have his moments such as at the U.S. Masters in 1978 when he won the title for a third time with an astonishing Palmer-type last round charge in which he birdied seven of the last ten holes. He did so alongside one Severiano Ballesteros, of whom much more would be heard, and he went on to complete a quite unique hat-trick by winning the Tournament of Champions, then the Houston Open.

This, however, was the era of Nicklaus. Two years after turning professional Nicklaus was, in

Right: Jack Nicklaus watches the course of his putt with intense concentration at Augusta.

1963, the second player to earn more than $100,000 in one season. The figure grew with his victories to more than $200,000 in 1971, more than $300,000 in 1973, and, as others took over the individual seasonal records, so Nicklaus was overall the leading money winner. Although in July 1968 Palmer became the first player to earn more than $1 million in official winnings on the U.S. Tour, Nicklaus was the first to make it to $2 million (December 1973), $3 million (May 1977), $4 million (February 1983), and then $5 million in 1987. Twelve years on Tiger Woods would earn $6 million in a single season!

Nicklaus's first U.S. Masters win had come in 1963 when, although five shots behind, he came through to get his first fitting of the famous green jacket, which was awarded annually to the custodian of the tournament. He followed that

performance later in the year by winning the U.S. P.G.A. Championship for the first time when he came home ahead of Dave Regan, Junior, at the Dallas Athletic Club in Texas. The old green jacket was his again in 1965 at Augusta National where he was in magnificent form. His first round of 67 put him two strokes behind Player. In the second round he drew level with Player and Palmer. Then it happened—he burst out of the field with a record 64 which included eight birdies, ten pars, and not a five in his card. His devastating drives, around the 300 yard mark, were power strokes of some magnitude. Nicklaus set a new record aggregate of 271, which would remain intact until beaten by Woods in 1997, and he won by a record margin of nine strokes.

It was not until his fifth assault on the Open Championship, at Muirfield in 1966, that he finally won this prized title. By then the prize money had increased by 20 per cent from the previous year when the Australian Peter Thomson had regained the silver claret jug following victories by New Zealand's Bob Charles and America's Tony Lema in 1963 and 1964.

Thomson's win in 1965 had been much deserved. Some had commented that by not taking on the best in the United States Thomson had himself highlighted a flaw in his universal ability. And that when he was winning Open Championships in the 1950s there were not many Americans in the field at the time to challenge him. It was also cruelly said of him that he had no taste for courses in the United States that were not suited to his style. That the larger American ball had less appeal to Thomson is almost certainly nearer the truth.

But Thomson needs no defense of his ability. It was there for all to see, including the American

Right: Jack Nicklaus at Augusta

National in 1986.

public, as he won the Texas Open in 1956. He was a highly skilled craftsman who compensated for his lack of length by scrambling with a highly adept touch. He played an active role in public life, his concern for others evident in his work for an antidrugs organization. In 1965 he answered his critics with a marvelous performance.

In 1966, however, the British public had a new champion. It was Nicklaus's turn and he won from his compatriot Doug Sanders and the Welshman David Thomas. Nicklaus was a true master from tee to green. His campaign for perfection often meant that he stood most of the day on the practice range. He would blister his hands hitting around 500 balls and consoled himself with the knowledge that it was turning him into the world's finest golfer.

Nicklaus's first Open Championship came in the same year that it was decided to play the event over four days instead of packing the final

two rounds into one day. Thus it was stretched through to the Saturday and the era of the true tournament professional had arrived. In the past it had been felt that most professionals would have to be back at their club posts for the weekend to cater to the members. Life was changing on the British fairways also as far as the professionals were concerned, although the massive increases in prize money would in reality not reach Europe until the 1980s.

Even so the Open Championship was now flourishing. Palmer had done his work and whereas before his arrival television coverage had consisted of barely one hour's play, by 1967 the A.B.C. T.V. company had purchased American rights as a forerunner to the Championship being screened to millions of viewers all over the world.

The victory of the popular Argentinian Roberto de Vicenzo was one to cherish in 1967

as he came home at Hoylake, although there was to be disappointment for him the following year when he lost the U.S. Masters by signing for a wrong score. Officials searched for a way out for Vicenzo, whose only crime had been to sign the card without checking it, but they were nevertheless compelled to abide by the rules of the game.

Nicklaus, of course, continued with his winning ways. Even so, players like Gay Brewer, Bob Goalby, who benefited at Vicenzo's expense, and George Archer took the U.S. Masters title in 1967, 1968, and 1969 respectively. It was the U.S. Open of 1968, however, that unearthed the first real challenger to Nicklaus's reign on the golfing throne.

His name was Lee Buck Trevino and with his rounds of 69, 68, 69, and 69 at Oak Hill, Rochester, New York, he became the first player in the history of the U.S. Open to play four sub-70 rounds. What is more he matched Nicklaus's one-year-old record aggregate for the U.S. Open of 275 and he pushed Nicklaus into the runner's-up berth. The Trevino story reads like a boys' adventure story. He came from the other side of the tracks in Dallas, Texas, to win not only fame but also a fortune on the fairways.

The kid was first introduced to golf around the age of seven when he helped out on a local golf range. The man who ran the place, Hardy Greenwood, set Lee on the way with a little push, a lot of guidance, and his first set of clubs. Lee stayed on at the range until he joined the U.S. Marine Corps. He served for about four years and then became the assistant in the professional shop at El Paso, Texas. This experience was to stand him in good stead later in life when on the road to golfing fame. He picked up the golf lingo and chit-chat, and his pleasing personality made him a natural hit wherever he played.

In 1965 he won the Texas State Open and began moving up. He finished fifth behind Nicklaus in the 1967 U.S. Open at Baltusrol, Springfield, New Jersey, and by this stage was playing the full tournament circuit. But it was at the U.S. Open the following year that he really made his mark. His opening two rounds put him five in the lead over Nicklaus. He was caught, however, and overtaken by Bert Yancey. What a contrasting sight they made. There was the laugh-a-minute Trevino, the stocky former gun sergeant, and Yancey, who had been a cadet at West Point and who was recognized for his classic swing. Not so for Trevino who went to work with an unorthodox open stance.

Trevino, however, started to chip away at Yancey's lead. It was not classic stuff in the last round but Trevino's putting was canceling any errors he made on the way to the green. Nicklaus had lost ground and with Yancey faltering so Lee Trevino was able to take the title.

It was at around this time on the other side of the Atlantic that another challenger to Nicklaus emerged. His name was Tony Jacklin. He was the son of a locomotive driver from Scunthorpe in England. His arrival would launch the golf boom in Britain and subsequently on the European continent. Jacklin was to enjoy a highly profitable career; his most cherished moments came at Royal Lytham and St. Annes in 1969 when he won the Open Championship, and at Hazeltine, Chaska, Minneapolis, 11 months later when he won the U.S. Open.

In between those wins came an historic and touching moment for both Jacklin and Nicklaus. It occurred in the autumn of 1969 at Royal

Left: Lee Trevino (left), golf's joker of the pack, provides the fans with something to laugh about as he explains to British comedian Bruce Forsyth how he missed a putt in 1971 at Royal Birkdale.

Far Right: Britain's Tony Jacklin in action in 1967.

Right: Lee Trevino's constant smile is banished for once by a difficult shot from trees during the 1984 U.S. Championship P.G.A. Tour.

Below Right: With his laugh-a-minute antics Trevino is a popular figure on the golfing circuit.

Right: Tony Jacklin at home with the U.S. Open trophy which he won in 1970 by seven shots from Dave Hill at Hazeltine Country Club.

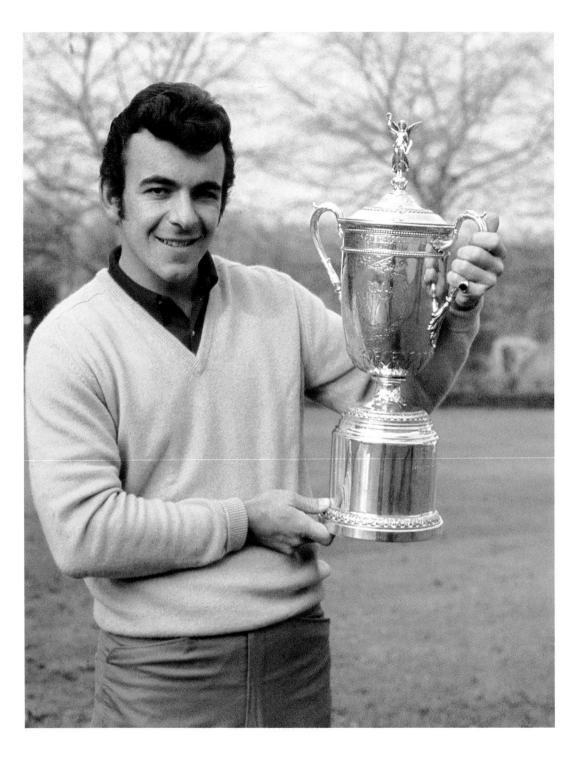

Birkdale, where Great Britain and Ireland were locked in battle with the United States for the Ryder Cup. The inaugural Ryder Cup contest had been held in 1927 although there had been a match at Gleneagles six years earlier when the Americans lost, and another informal affair in 1926. After four official matches the overall score stood at 2-2.

By the time the 1969 match unfolded it was 14-3 in the United States' favor!

Jacklin and Nicklaus would have other scraps, as opposing captains in the Ryder Cup but their duel as players at Royal Birkdale will live long in the memory of all those who witnessed it. On the last green Nicklaus moved quickly over to Jacklin's ball marker, which was some three

feet from the hole, and he picked it up. With that generous gesture he ensured that for the first time in the history of the match the result would be a tie.

What is more, it was the kind of sporting act that would win Nicklaus support in Britain. He had won his first battle, against the army of fans who cheered Palmer and jeered him, and he now wanted to endorse that feeling across the Atlantic. He went much of the way that afternoon on the Lancashire coast, but it was surely at St. Andrews in 1970 that he won the day.

Nicklaus had not won a major championship since the U.S. Open in 1967. Billy Casper had beaten Gene Littler in a play-off for the U.S. Masters earlier in 1970 after which Jacklin had

Above: The view over the 18th hole to the club house at Royal Birkdale.

become the first British winner of the U.S. Open since Ted Ray in 1920. With such results, plus the emergence of Trevino, there was a threat to Nicklaus. Like all great stars he was being placed under increasing pressure through his absence from the winners' circle of the championships that really matter.

He was helped at St. Andrews in that summer of 1970 when Doug Sanders took three putts—missing from three feet—on the last green. This produced a tie and Nicklaus won the

play-off by playing the last hole in great style. He peeled off his sweater, hit an almighty drive, and the ball actually went over the green. But he chipped back down to six feet, then holed for a birdie that kept him ahead of Sanders with a 72 to a 73.

Jacklin had covered the opening nine holes in the first round that year at St. Andrews in 29 strokes. It was an amazing start to a title defense, but he was sabotaged by a thunderstorm. Play was stopped and when Jacklin returned the following day the magic had left his game. He might have won again in 1971, but Trevino triumphed. In 1972 at Muirfield Trevino ended Jacklin's brief challenge to Nicklaus for world supremacy by twice holing out in the third round, then providing the ultimate in killing blows at the 17th on the final day. Lee said later, "God is a Mexican!"

It seemed that Jacklin, on the green in three at the par five and only 15 feet from the hole, was ready to win again. Then Trevino, who had virtually given up all hope of winning, contrived to chip in from off the green for the unlikeliest of par fives while Jacklin three putted for a six. Killer shots such as these can deliver such a psychological blow to a player that they can unnerve him completely. That happened to Jacklin who would no longer be the force that he had once been.

Trevino, however, was doing his level best to push Nicklaus to one side. He had a marvelous set-to with Nicklaus in the U.S. Open at Merion in 1971 where they finished level. Trevino won the play-off with a 68 to a 71 and, laughing and joking throughout, he named Nicklaus the world's best golfer.

After his success at Muirfield, Trevino won two U.S. Opens and two British Opens as well as the first of his two U.S. P.G.A. Championships—the other came during a revival in 1984—at Tanglewood, Winston-Salem, North Carolina in 1974.

At the Western Open in 1975, however, Trevino was struck by lightning—he was thankful that his life was spared—and from that moment he was bugged with back trouble. Trevino was not a quitter and he soldiered on despite a rapid decline. Then in 1984 "Super Mex," as he is fondly known, came back to win the U.S. P.G.A.

Championship again at Shoal Creek, Birmingham, Alabama, with Player and Lanny Wadkins sharing the runner's-up spot.

It was no less than he deserved. Lee Trevino had added a smile to the face of competitive golf. His sense of humor, like donning a top hat and tails in Britain at the start of the Alcan Golfer of the Year Tournament at a time when there was talk about his dress sense, was like a breath of fresh air. He had a marvelous rapport with the galleries of spectators that few, if any, have ever equaled. It is said that it is best to laugh at life. Lee continues to laugh at golf—at what it did for him and what he did for it.

Nicklaus, however, remained the king as the seventies unfolded. He had dethroned Palmer, kept Player at arm's length and parried the thrusts of Jacklin and Trevino. Yet there were bigger battles to be fought by the man who was now loved by the spectators everywhere. The "Golden Bear," as he was now known, would have to huff and puff and blow a few more challengers away.

THE POWER STUGGLE

Right: Johnny Miller, who came from
nowhere to claim international
stardom in the 1970s. During that
time his golf was of a standard that
very few players in the history of
the game have attained.

The seventies would see a dazzling display of stirring performances from Jack Nicklaus. He won in 1971, apart from the U.S. P.G.A. Championship, four other events on the American circuit including the national team title with Arnold Palmer. In 1972 he took seven titles, including the U.S. Masters and the U.S. Open, and there were to be seven victories again in 1973. These included the U.S. P.G.A. Championship—one month after he had finished fourth in the Open Championship at Royal Troon behind Tom Weiskopf and Johnny Miller.

The persistence of Nicklaus would face two new rivals in Miller, who had won the U.S. Open earlier in 1973 at Oakmont, and Weiskopf. At Troon, Weiskopf had overcome the wet conditions to register an important win whereas Miller, newer to the scene, was about to set the U.S. Tour alight with no fewer than eight wins in 1974—including the first three of the season—as he rocketed to number one in the official money list.

Miller had first gained national notoriety when, after signing up to caddie at the 1966 U.S. Open at the Olympic Club in his home town of San Francisco, he actually qualified to compete. He eventually finished joint eighth. It was not until the 1973 U.S. Open, however, that he earned global respect when he achieved a sparkling last round of 63.

Miller, the golden boy from California, had claimed stardom with a powerful and precise game coupled with a wonderful touch on the greens. He had, in one sense, emerged from nowhere. In contrast Weiskopf's success at Troon only cemented the belief that here was the man with the finest swing in golf at the time, a swing both smooth and predictable. Perhaps because he was born in Ohio, Weiskopf was seen as a rival to Nicklaus who also came from that state. In fact it was a comparison which did Weiskopf little good for at times he came under a great deal of pressure because of the association.

Even so, with Nicklaus not winning a major championship in 1974—Gary Player took the U.S. Masters and the Open Championship, Hale Irwin the U.S. Open at Winged Foot, Mamaroneck, New York, and Lee Trevino the U.S. P.G.A. Championship at Tanglewood, North Carolina—Miller and Weiskopf were regarded as the new breed. Nicklaus, however, emphasized at Augusta in the spring of 1975 that he was ready to meet their challenge. The "Golden Bear," now much loved by the American public, flourished amid the azaleas and the dogwood to score an emphatic victory in the U.S. Masters.

It was a classic ding-dong encounter all the way. Nicklaus departed from his usual practice of launching last round charges to lead the way with opening rounds of 68 and 67. In the third round, however, he faltered by taking 73. Miller, 11 shots behind at the halfway stage, could thus pick up eight of these with a 65. Meanwhile, Weiskopf edged ahead of Nicklaus with a 66. The scene was

Far Left: Tom Weiskopf kisses the trophy as he basks in the glory of being the 1973 Open champion following a fine performance at Royal Troon.

Far Left Below: Weiskopf as part of the 1973 U.S. Ryder Cup team at Muirfield.

Left: Weiskopf demonstrating a stylish swing that helped win him the 1973 Open Championship.

Right: Californian golden boy Johnny Miller at the Open Championship at Troon in 1973 where he tied second with Neil Coles behind Tom Weiskopf. Miller returned to win in 1976.

set for a quite extraordinary final day during which any one of these three players might have won. Miller's outward 32, including five birdies, was the stuff of champions. Weiskopf, however, remained in front. He was paired with Miller, and Nicklaus was playing ahead.

Nicklaus, however, seemed to hold the upper hand as, with six holes remaining, he led by one from Weiskopf with Miller a further two shots adrift. Miller was the only one of the three to extract a birdie from the long 13th. Nicklaus dropped a shot at the 14th and Weiskopf, playing the hole some ten minutes later, made a birdie. Weiskopf was back in the lead but Nicklaus made a birdie at the long 15th, hitting a superb one iron into the heart of the green. It seemed likely to be a crucial blow when Weiskopf's approach skipped over the green but he chipped back to 15 feet

from where he holed for a birdie. It kept him ahead at 12 under par, with Nicklaus in hot competition at 11 under and Miller, who had also birdied the 15th, now at ten under.

There comes a time, however, in any sport when an individual becomes a true champion of the game. This was Nicklaus's moment. Weiskopf had every right to feel, as he walked onto the 16th tee, that he was at last going to win a championship by extinguishing Nicklaus's flame. He looked ahead and he could see that Nicklaus was some 40 feet from the hole. Nicklaus could three putt from there.

Then came the moment of reality for Weiskopf. Nicklaus hit his putt and the ball raced toward the cup. Then it disappeared and, as Nicklaus extended his putter high above his head in a gesture of delight, so Weiskopf was aware

Left: Hale Irwin won the Piccadilly World Match-Play Championship in successive years in 1974 and 1975 at Wentworth, England.

that the initiative had swung back into the hands of his rival. Weiskopf waited, hoping to retain the level-headed confidence he now required, but his shot came up some 35 yards short. He took three to get down.

It wasn't over—although, perhaps, in retrospect it was. Miller, as he was inclined to do in such situations, made a birdie at the 17th so that both he and Weiskopf now required a birdie at the last to tie with Nicklaus. Weiskopf struck at that 18th hole that travels uphill toward the cloistered Augusta clubhouse, a prodigious drive. He had hit the ball about 50 yards past Miller and he needed only a nine iron for his approach. Miller, playing first, hit his shot to 20 feet; Weiskopf, as if under no pressure whatsoever, struck his to ten feet. Nicklaus, however, had done enough. He was in the clubhouse and the pressure was on his opponents to hole their putts. They failed. And Nicklaus became the Five Star Champion of the Masters Tournament. Weiskopf, for a fourth time, had finished in the runner's-up spot. The glory of Augusta would never be his and Nicklaus had seen to it that another of his challengers had been compelled to accept defeat.

To his eternal credit Miller would take on Nicklaus once more in the Open Championship at Royal Birkdale in 1976. This time he would win, with Nicklaus forced to accept a share of second place along with a precocious Spaniard called Severiano Ballesteros. It would appear to the majority of observers that the era of Miller had begun.

That, however, was not to be. Instead Tom Watson, a young, freckle-faced kid from Kansas City who became known as the Huckleberry Finn of golf, offered Nicklaus a new challenge. He

had revealed to British spectators that he possessed a solid game and an efficient, almost mechanical, putting method, by winning the Open Championship at Carnoustie in 1975. There he had beaten Jack Newton, the Australian, with a 71 to a 72 in a play-off. Watson endeared himself to the British public because he belonged to that enviable breed who get on with the game without making any fuss or bother. When a shot finished in a bunker, he even smiled, showing he was human.

Watson had started out, like so many other youngsters, by being introduced to the game by his father. Tom, born in Kansas City in September 1949, was six years old at the time and his father was a scratch golfer. The young Watson was quick to respond to tuition and he went on to become a four-times winner of the Missouri State Amateur and to play for three years at Stanford University, before graduating in 1971 with a degree in psychology.

Watson turned professional in 1972 and slowly but surely he began to make his mark on the game. The trouble for American observers, even after Watson's win in the Western Open on the brutal Butler National course in 1974, was in deciding whether or not he was a bona fide challenger. Yes, he had won at Carnoustie, but no, he had lost the U.S. Opens of 1974 and 1975—Hale Irwin and Lou Graham had won after being in challenging positions. Some had cruelly chosen to call Watson a "choker," a reference to the fact that he was unable to stand up to the pressure.

The Open Championship, however, had at least provided a launch pad for Watson. He was convinced that if he could win at Carnoustie then he could win other major championships. What is more he also won the World Series of Golf in

1975 which, although only a four-man series then, included the cream of the game. Yet it was not until 1977 that it really began to happen for Watson. First he won the U.S. Masters, earning a stream of complimentary remarks about his future, notably from Nicklaus, and then he went head-to-head with Nicklaus for the Open Championship at Turnberry in one of the most fascinating encounters in the history of golf.

Coincidentally, when Nicklaus put down the challenges of Miller and Weiskopf in the 1975 U.S.

Masters, his playing partner on the final day was none other than Tom Sturges Watson. That taste of the power and the glory of the game had driven Watson, two months later, into a clear lead in the U.S. Open at Medinah, where, however, he would finish with rounds of 78 and 77, hence the "choker" reputation.

If there was any truth in that reputation then surely at Augusta in 1977 Watson should have taken five at the 11th instead of chipping to two feet, saving his par, after watching Nicklaus who

Above: Tom Watson and his wife celebrate his 1975 win at the Open Championship held at Carnoustie. He had beaten the Australian Jack Newton with a 71 to a 72 in a nail-biting play-off.

165

was ahead of him, close to within one shot with a 12 foot birdie putt at the short 12th. The challenge was on and Nicklaus seemed to suggest so when he tapped in for a birdie four at the long 13th. Watson was standing in the middle of the fairway at the time waiting to play his next shot and Nicklaus, leaving the green, raised his arm and looked back down the fairway. There were many at that moment—including Watson—who viewed that as a challenging gesture. Nicklaus insisted later that he would never do such a thing and Watson accepted Nicklaus's explanation and apologized for thinking that he might.

Nevertheless it heightened the drama at the time. Watson felt his lips dry. He knew this was the moment, that the last hour on this great golf course could possibly decide his place in the game. If he could beat Nicklaus now then he would erase that "choker" image. He wasn't worried by it but he could not ignore it. And what better place to prove his ability to the doubting Thomases than Augusta.

Sadly, Bobby Jones was not there to see this great drama unfold but if he had been then surely he would, like the rest of those who were present, have congratulated Watson. For as early as

Above: Tom Watson getting out of a bunker during practice for the 1981 Ryder Cup.

Left: A grinning Jack Newton knows that he has made a great approach shot during the final day of action at the 1978 Buick Open. Newton became the winner in a sudden death play-off with Mike Sullivan.

1965 Jones had declared: "Jack Nicklaus plays a game of which I am not familiar." It was a reference to his admiration for Nicklaus and that admiration would have extended to any player who was capable of taking on and then beating the formidable "Golden Bear."

Watson, however, looked as if he might crumble when he took five at the 14th, so losing the outright lead. Moreover Nicklaus extracted a birdie four from the long 15th to go one ahead as revealed by the giant leader boards of Augusta. Watson, however, reached the 15th with a drive and a two iron and he putted for a birdie, as Nicklaus parred the 16th ahead of him. In fact it was not until Nicklaus stood in the middle of the 18th fairway that another huge roar ascended

from the spectators as those standing near the 17th watched Watson's birdie from 20 feet topple into the cup. It was a deafening blow for Nicklaus. The great champion hit behind his ball with a six iron and the ball finished short of the green in a bunker. The duel was over and Watson, the David of the piece, had slain the Goliath of golf.

The talk across the length and breadth of the United States was of Nicklaus and Watson meeting head-to-head again in the U.S. Open at Southern Hills, Tulsa, Oklahoma. This was not to be, for there Hubert Green outlasted Lou Graham. Even so the golfing populace did not have to wait long. Nicklaus and Watson would, like two golfing gunfighters, duel again that

Above: The view of the lighthouse over the 11th green at Turnberry on Scotland's west coast.

Left: Tom Watson celebrates on the 18th green at Turnberry where he was victorious in the 1977 Open Championship following a titanic battle with Jack Nicklaus.

Above: Tom Watson (center) and Jack Nicklaus (left) shelter from the storm during their classic duel at Turnberry.

summer at Turnberry for the Open Championship. The event was a classic.

The Royal and Ancient had chosen in 1977 to put Turnberry on the map. It would join the Open Championship rota along with Carnoustie, St. Andrews, Muirfield, and Royal Troon in Scotland, and Royal Birkdale, Royal Lytham and St. Annes, and Royal St. George's in England. For Turnberry it was quite a miracle that golf was being played there.

Even before the evolution of golf the countryside had been scarred by the battles of yesteryear with kings like Robert the Bruce defending their castles. The events of the Second World War, when tarmac strips were laid across Turnberry's springy turf so spoiling the courses, were even more damaging to the countryside.

Following the war, the Scottish architect Mackenzie Ross helped repair the course at Turnberry and this now became the arena for what many people regard as the most exciting Open Championship in the history of the sport.

All eyes were trained from the start on Jack Nicklaus, the "King," and Tom Watson, the

"Crown Prince." Yet few could have predicted, as they both opened with rounds of 68 and 70, what would eventually unfold. These two supreme golfers simply engaged in a fascinating duel. Nicklaus first in front, then Watson coming back, and for the excited spectators it was quite magical entertainment. Only a thunderstorm would interrupt them during a sweltering third day. Nicklaus and Watson sought refuge among the rocks, and this provided a brief interlude for the two golfers to ponder the situation or look out to sea to Ailsa Craig, a rocky islet in the Firth of Clyde, and to the peaks of Arran. Then it was back to business as the two golfers kept the tension running high when they completed 65s to remain locked in the lead.

The sun shone on Turnberry on that final day and on Nicklaus for the first four holes. By that time he had moved three strokes ahead and it seemed he was out for a stroll. Watson, however, had won his badge of courage three months earlier at Augusta. He could now digest such turnarounds and, more important, he could come back. He birdied the fifth, seventh, and eighth, and as the spectators rushed from hole to hole, the officials were compelled to call a short halt. When play resumed Watson bogeyed the ninth and was one behind again. Nicklaus's 25 foot birdie putt at the 12th gave him a two-stroke lead.

Watson retaliated with a putt of 12 feet for a birdie at the 13th. He turned to Nicklaus, remarking "Is this what it's all about, Jack?" Back came the answer, swift and succinct, "Right, Tom." Nicklaus, still one ahead, naturally knew that the unpredictable nature of the game meant that this Open Championship was far from over. However, he can be forgiven for feeling, even today, that

he was robbed of the initiative by an audacious stroke at the 15th. There Watson rolled the ball in from 60 feet for a two. The shot gave Watson the momentum to go on and birdie the 17th, so that in three holes he had come from one behind to one ahead at the most crucial time in the match.

The game must have seemed a foregone conclusion at the 18th when Watson drilled a magnificent seven-iron approach to within 18 inches of the flag. Nicklaus's second had finished some 30 feet away from the cup. He would need to hole that to put pressure on Watson. The odds against doing so must have been heavily stacked against him, but in the ball went. The gallery could hardly believe it.

Now Watson had to make his putt. It still measured only 18 inches in length but as Nicklaus accepted the applause of the congregation so Watson must have felt in his heart that the putt was growing longer all the time. But he made no mistake and the title was really his at last

It had been the classic to beat all classics. Watson had fired a last round of 65 to Nicklaus's 66 and he had won the second of his five Open Championships. If any one player truly challenged Nicklaus when he was at the height of his game, then it must be Watson. He set new standards and smashed records, emerging on no less than six occasions between 1977 and 1984 as player of the year in the United States and five times the leading money winner.

Watson was also to win the U.S. Masters again in 1981 although he must have gained greater satisfaction with his U.S. Open success at Pebble Beach in 1982. There, on the Californian coast, it was almost like Turnberry revisited.

Left: A beautiful view of hole seven at Pebble Beach, California where the 2000 U.S. Open was held.

This time Nicklaus and Watson were not paired together and it was Nicklaus who finished first. He shot a last round of 69—an excellent performance on the Pebble Beach course which is regarded by many golfing experts as the eighth wonder of the world. This meant that Watson would need to make a birdie at one of the two remaining holes. That seemed most unlikely to Nicklaus as he signed his card. For the news was that Watson had missed the green at the short 17th. He faced the prospect of taking four, since his ball was buried in a collar of grass between two bunkers. There was only 30 feet between him and the hole but it seemed impossible for Watson to get the ball close. The ball would, however, come out of that ankle-deep rough fast and, with only 12 feet of green with which to work, this was one of those 10,000-1 make-or-break shots. Such was Watson's confidence that, as his caddie, hoping to inspire his employer, whispered, "Get it close, Tom," so he replied, "I'll do better than that—I'll make it!"

Players of Watson's class immediately know when they have executed the perfect shot. As he knocked the ball toward the hole Watson yelled, "It's going in—I know it's going in!" It did, and Nicklaus, deflated, observed, "Tom could have gone back there and hit that shot one thousand times and he would not have made it."

A dream for Nicklaus had been dashed. He had hoped at Pebble Beach to win a record fifth U.S. Open which would push him ahead of Anderson, Hogan, and Jones. Nicklaus would have to wait until 1986 for another major championship, although when it came, at Augusta, he would not only establish another record with a sixth U.S. Masters title but would unquestionably prove that he could still put down those "upstarts" who assumed they could relieve him of the number one tag.

Watson had made a gallant effort and with his Open Championship win at Royal Birkdale in 1983 he did move to within one more victory of equaling Harry Vardon's record of six successes. Nicklaus will never make that total but who will ever match Nicklaus's achievement in winning six U.S. Masters, five U.S. P.G.A. Championships, four U.S. Opens, three U.S. Masters, and two U.S. Amateur Championships? Tiger Woods? Maybe, but we must wait and see.

Others have tried. The gospel of golf had spread to such an extent that as Nicklaus and Watson dueled for supremacy so the scene was also enlivened by the arrival of newcomers such as Severiano Ballesteros and José Maria Olazábal of Spain, Bernhard Langer of Germany, Greg Norman of Australia, Nick Price of Zimbabwe, and the British golfers Nick Faldo, Sandy Lyle, and Ian Woosnam in addition to a host of talented Americans including Curtis Strange and Payne Stewart.

The popularity of golf owes much to the intense coverage provided by television and other media. Knowledge of the game was initially limited to a chosen few and it should be remembered that the first official golf tour took place only in 1903 when the Oxford and Cambridge Golfing Society went to the United States.

What is more, while there might have been championships in places such as Australia and South Africa during the 1900s, it was not until the 1930s that the game of golf made spectacular progress. The game that had been created by the Scots or the Dutch—depending on which historians you choose to believe—was most

Left: Ian Woosnam, pictured here at the 1987 World Match-Play Championship, became a prolific winner after breaking through with his 1982 Swiss Open win. By the start of 2000 he had captured 43 titles worldwide including the 1991 U.S. Masters.

Right: Sandy Lyle kisses the Open
Championship trophy which he won
in 1985—three years later he was
the U.S. Masters champion.

Left: Seve Ballesteros of Spain finished joint runner-up with Jack Nicklaus at his first Open Championship in 1976 at the age of just 19.

certainly popularized by the Americans. As world travel became easier and cheaper, so American golfers extended their influence to other parts of the globe, with the result that players such as Palmer began to encourage the building of golf courses in places as far afield as China. There, with his architect Ed Seay, he laid out in 1982 the Chung Shan Hot Spring golf course. China was back on the golfing map for the first time since 1949, when golf had been decreed a bourgeois pastime and the few courses that existed had been turned into paddy fields.

The likes of Player and Locke, from South Africa, Nagle and Thomson, from Australia, Bob Charles from New Zealand, and Roberto de Vicenzo from Argentina, gave golf a truly international flavor. Yet it was not until such golfers as Ballesteros and Langer, Lyle and Norman, Faldo and Price, that Americans faced a truly serious threat to their supremacy in world

Right: Seve Ballesteros raises the silver claret jug high at the 1984 Open Championship at St Andrews.

golf. Gary Player remains probably the finest example of a non-American to compete successfully around the world. David Graham of Australia, too, has a fine record, with the 1979 U.S. P.G.A. Championship and the 1981 U.S. Open to his credit. Greg Norman is a further example of a golfer all the way from Down Under whose performance has been astonishing. In 1986 Norman won the Open Championship at Turnberry and later that year he finished at the top of the U.S. Tour money list. To take on the cream of American golf week by week and to become the first "overseas" winner of the official money list since Gary Player in 1961 is a very impressive and laudable achievement.

Yet even though Nicklaus held a high regard for Norman from the moment they first played together it had already become apparent in these changing times, with the globe shrinking as Concorde whisked air travelers across the Atlantic in three hours, that Ballesteros was now the "man" as he took on Nicklaus, Watson, and company in their own backyard. The Spaniard sharpened his claws against the "Golden Bear" by pushing Nicklaus into joint second place in the Open Championship at Royal Lytham and St. Annes in 1979 and it was Watson who had to accept that position at St. Andrews in 1984.

Ballesteros ushered in a new era. The young golfer from the north coast of Spain soon showed that he was the most exciting prospect since Arnold Palmer. As a 19-year-old he captured the imagination of the world with his brave bid to win the Open Championship at Royal Birkdale. After three rounds he took the lead, and, in spite of eventually finishing joint runner-up with Nicklaus behind Miller, he was here to stay.

Later, in 1976, Ballesteros linked with his compatriot, Manuel Pinero, to win the World Cup for Spain—pushing the American combination of Jerry Pate who had won the U.S. Open that summer at the Atlanta Athletic Club in Georgia, and Dave Stockton, the reigning U.S. P.G.A. champion, into second place at Mission Hills, California.

So two unknown Spaniards had hammered out an early warning to American golf. There was a revolutionary move in Europe with players on

the continent emerging to challenge for the big prizes on offer in golf. That Ballesteros and Pinero should win the World Cup was quite remarkable. For instance Pinero, born in Badajoz near the Portuguese border, was a product of the caddie schools. His father was a pig farmer but when times became hard the family moved to Madrid and so Pinero found his way to the Club de Campo course where he could earn a few pesetas to supplement the family income.

In Spain the game of golf was known only to the aristocracy who played at sophisticated clubs and to the children of impoverished families who turned up to caddie. The origins of the game in Spain can be traced to British architects but the sport was virtually a private, exclusive pastime. The taxi-driver and the shop worker, the hotelier and the motor mechanic, knew nothing of the sport. For them the major pastimes were football and bullfighting.

The likes of Pinero, however, profited by working at golf clubs. On occasions they were allowed to borrow clubs from the members and so hone their own games. Even so it required enormous strength of character to survive. Yet there was an instinctive quality about the golf of some of these continental players. Ballesteros personifies this best although he had the advantage of coming from a golfing background. His uncle Ramon had proved himself to be a golfer of high regard by winning six Opens around the world. If you thumb your way back through the record books then you will see that in 1965 Ramon Sota succeeded in finishing sixth in the U.S. Masters behind Jack Nicklaus!

Ballesteros had more than just background going for him. He had inherited an athletic ability from his father who, apart from being a fine long

Right: This photograph of Seve
Ballesteros at the 1988 Open
Championship shows just how much
concentration and effort the golfer
puts into his strokes. Ballesteros
won the title for a third time that
year, and his spectacular career
was superbly recognized in 2000
with the playing of the inaugural
Eurobet Seve Ballesteros Trophy at
Sunningdale, Berkshire, England.
Continental Europe captained by
Seve, beat Great Britain and Ireland
13½ – 12½ with Ballesteros beating
Colin Montgomerie, the G.B. and
Ireland captain, in the top singles of
a match likened to the Ryder Cup.

distance runner, rowed on several occasions in the Pedrena boat that won national championships in annual matches around Santander Bay. More importantly the Ballesteros home—a 19th century farmhouse—overlooked the Real Club de Golf de Pedrena, and his brothers, Baldomero, Manuel, and Vicente, were all golfers. Even so it was far from easy for Ballesteros to develop his game.

For instance Seve hit his first shots at the age of seven with a club fashioned from a rusting three-iron head hand-fitted into a stick acting as a shaft. His ammunition? Stones that he collected from the nearby beach—golf balls were too expensive for one so young. Ballesteros, like so many Spaniards who were to make a living from golf, initially caddied to earn his keep. Then at the age of ten he played in his first event. It was held over nine holes and Ballesteros carded a 51.

Two years later he had become the caddie champion at Pedrena with the impressive score of 79. In 1973 he was once again the caddie champion although on this occasion he managed a score of 65. There was to be no stopping him and in January 1974 at the age of 16 years and eight months he became the youngest accredited professional in the history of Spanish golf.

What Ballesteros did was to assume the role of challenger to American golfers on their own soil. He was soon winning abroad and in 1977 he claimed both the Japanese Open and the Dunlop Phoenix, also staged in Japan. Ballesteros was hailed as a king in Japan where the interest in golf had been fueled by Japan's World Cup victory in 1957, whereas the success of Ballesteros and Pinero did not have an immediate impact on the game in Spain. There the likes of Ballesteros would have to resort to gimmicky productions such as hitting balls over the stands at the Bernabeu Stadium, the home of the Real Madrid Football Club, so as to spread the word to the populace. The public were admitted free of charge to their special organized golf clinics.

In Japan the sport flourished even if many of those attracted to the game would never hit a golf ball on a course. Quite simply many of the millions of golf enthusiasts would be confined to the driving ranges because they could not afford the huge entry fees to the prospering private clubs.

Ballesteros, of course, enjoyed his victories in Japan. But in 1978 he scored a far more significant success across the Pacific Ocean when, to acclimatize himself for the U.S. Masters, he accepted an invitation to compete in the Greater Greensboro Open in North Carolina. There was something Nicklaus-like in the manner in which Ballesteros, who survived the halfway cut by only one shot, came from ten strokes behind with rounds of 69 and 66 to win by one from Jack Renner and Fuzzy Zoeller, who would win the U.S. Masters one year later.

The impact that Ballesteros made in the United States cannot be over-exaggerated. The following week at Augusta he was partnered on the last day with Gary Player who put together 64 that would win him the Championship. The next, at the Tournament of Champions, Ballesteros sped into the halfway lead only to falter with a closing 79 which enabled Player to come through and snatch victory once again.

Player went on to win the Houston Open to complete a rare hat-trick. That streak, however, would be the start of the decline of Player's phenomenal career. He would not win again on the regular U.S. Tour although he would reign

Right: Tom Kite launched a "new" career on the U.S. Seniors Tour when he won The Tradition, beating Tom Watson and Larry Nelson in a play-off, in the year 2000. This followed an outstanding record on the regular tour which included winning the 1992 U.S. Open.

supreme as a new circuit—the U.S. Seniors Tour. It was Ballesteros who had now grasped the baton. In 1980 he became only the second overseas golfer—following in Player's footsteps—to win the U.S. Masters, and he did so with the greatest of ease. He was four ahead at the halfway stage, seven in front after 54 holes, and no fewer than 16 under par with a ten-shot lead midway through the final round. Eventually he won by only four shots—Gibby Gilbert and

Australia's Jack Newton shared second spot—but it was still a masterful performance. He had become at the age of 23 the youngest champion at that time in the history of the Masters. What is more he won the title again in 1983 when he accelerated away from Ben Crenshaw and Tom Kite in the final round to win by four shots.

What Ballesteros did with his smash-and-grab raids in the United States the Australian Greg Norman matched with his more orthodox approach. Norman elected to play full time on the U.S. circuit although it has to be emphasized that he married an American and that he found it easier to settle and live in Florida. The hardest aspect of a professional golfer's life is travel, and Ballesteros spent much of his time playing in his native Europe. Norman played on the European circuit for several seasons, heading the Order of

Merit in 1982, before he decided it was time to move on to the U.S. Tour.

Norman possessed all the attributes to become the master of Augusta National but, rather like Weiskopf, the golfing gods did not smile on him at this famous American course. Even so Ballesteros had with his wins in 1980 and 1983 at Augusta provided the inspiration for the overseas players, notably from Europe, to chase the power and the glory amongst the azaleas and the dogwood. In winning the U.S. Masters in 1985 Bernhard Langer of Germany proved himself a golfer of world class. There he became only the third foreign player at that time to wear the green jacket.

Langer's progress illustrated how public attitudes toward golf were changing. He recalls that in 1972 he announced to his friends that he

Right: Greg Norman sizes up a putt at Augusta National, but the Masters Tournament was always a finger-touch away for the Australian despite the fact that he had won more than 70 titles worldwide before the new millennium dawned.

wanted to become a professional golfer. "They thought I was mad and they had every right too," said Langer. "Even then I hardly knew of the existence of people like Jack Nicklaus and Arnold Palmer!"

That is hardly surprising. Bernhard, the son of a bricklayer, was born in the hamlet of Anheusen which at the time had a population of 1,200. His father Erwin, one of the millions of refugees from Sudetenland in Czechoslovakia, was caught by Russians and put on a train which, presumably, was heading for Siberia. "He jumped the train," explained Bernhard. "They shot at him, but they missed, and he walked all the way to Germany."

Bernhard, the youngest of three children, became a caddie at the age of nine at the Augsburg course in the village of Burgwalden. Langer possessed, however, that quality called ambition. To improve his own game he made sure that he caddied for the club champion. Then he moved on to be the assistant professional at Munich before joining the European Tour.

What threatened to end Langer's career before it had started was an attack of a putting yips. Call it the twitch, if you like, but this dreaded affliction which usually occurs in later life is the "disease" that all golfers fear. That Langer exorcized the demon from his game was in itself a minor miracle. There have been occasions when they have returned to haunt him, but at Augusta where the greens are recognized

to be the fastest in the world, he proved he could cope by winning the U.S. Masters.

Nicklaus, at the age of 46, was to relieve Langer of the title in 1986, then two months later Raymond Floyd, at 43, became the oldest winner at that time of the U.S. Open. In a curious way these events highlighted the situation in which golf now found itself. Greg Norman and Bob Tway, a 27-year-old from Oklahoma City, were to score their first major championship successes in the Open Championship and the U.S. P.G.A. Championship respectively. Even so it seemed that the time when a single player could dominate the game of golf had, perhaps, passed, albeit Ballesteros had by this time won four major championships to challenge Watson's eight and there appeared more to come from both.

Above: Greg Norman plays out of a bunker during the play off at the 1989 Open Championship at Royal Troon. Mark Calcavecchia won, beating Wayne Grady and Norman.

Above: Bernhard Langer of Germany holes a crucial putt during the 1985 Ryder Cup at The Belfry where he beat Hal Sutton 5 and 4 as Europe triumphed for the first time since 1957.

Ballesteros revived his hopes when he won the Open Championship in 1988 at Royal Lytham and St. Annes, where he had triumphed in 1979, but as golf hurtled towards the 1990s so Ballesteros and Watson were to find success increasingly elusive at the highest level. Indeed Watson would go from 1987 to 1996 without winning on the U.S. Tour and his hopes of winning more majors were frustrated too often by a disobedient putter.

There were new "faces" on the fairways. Craig Stadler, Ben Crenshaw, and Larry Mize won Masters titles in the 1980s with Mize denying Norman at Augusta National in 1987 by virtue of holing a 140-yards pitch shot at the second extra hole. Britain's Sandy Lyle, too, contributed to

Augusta's rich history of championship winning shots when he recovered in 1988 from a fairway bunker with a seven iron then holed a nine foot putt to beat Mark Calcavecchia by one shot. By now Lyle, who had become at Royal St. George's in 1985 the first British winner of the Open Championship since Tony Jacklin in 1969, was considered to be challenging Ballesteros and Langer as the best player in Europe.

The Americans, however, continued to dominate the major championships. Australian David Graham had won the U.S. Open at Merion in 1981, but Watson's victory at Pebble Beach in 1982, when he chipped in at the 17th for a birdie two to beat Nicklaus, had been followed by successes for Larry Nelson (1983), Fuzzy Zoeller

(1984), Andy North (1985), Ray Floyd (1986), and Scott Simpson (1987). Bill Rogers (1981) and Mark Calcavecchia (1989) were American winners of the Open Championship and compatriots Larry Nelson (1981 and 1987), Ray Floyd (1982), Hal Sutton (1983), Lee Trevino (1984), Hubert Green (1985), Bob Tway (1986), and Jeff Sluman (1988) kept the U.S. P.G.A. Championship at home.

Even so as a new decade arrived so the golfing world looked toward two other Americans, Payne Stewart and Curtis Strange, and one Englishman, Nick Faldo, to be the new role models. Faldo had been a professional for ten years, striving to find the swing that would give him the success he craved, before he struck

glory at Muirfield in 1987 when he captured the Open Championship ahead of America's Paul Azinger and Australia's Rodger Davis. Then he not only won the U.S. Masters in 1989 but one year later he successfully defended the Masters and won the Open Championship again. He would win the Open again in 1992 and in 1996 the Masters with a last round of 67, coming from six shots behind, to Norman's 78 to win by five—becoming the sixth player to win three times or more at Augusta National.

In those times there were those who regarded Faldo as the most complete golfer since Hogan. This was not far from the truth. Faldo had not set out to imitate Hogan, but it was in his nature to do so. He had been driven by ambition,

Above: Bernhard Langer photographed during the 1999 Italian Open at Torino which was won by Scotland's Dean Robertson.

Above: An exultant Larry Mize, having just chipped in at the second play-off hole at the 1987 U.S. Masters where he beat Seve Ballesteros and Greg Norman.

rather than avarice, since his teenage days when an obsession for golf began after he watched Jack Nicklaus on television during the school holidays in 1957, and, though labeled a loner, he determined that he would be the best in the business. His amateur career, during which he won the

English Championship at Royal Lytham and St. Annes in 1975, had earned for him due recognition, and when soon after turning professional he won both his matches with Peter Oosterhuis in the Ryder Cup then overcame Tom Watson in the singles there was little doubt that he

Above: Scotland's Sandy Lyle at Augusta in 1987. He would return the following year to win with a great bunker shot followed by a nine foot putt.

Left: The spectators watch as the action unfurls on the green at the 1986 U.S. Open, which took place at Shinnecock Hill, Long Island, and was won by Ray Floyd.

Right: Bill Rogers claimed a place in the record books when he won the Open Championship in 1981 at Royal St George's when Bernhard Langer finished runner-up.

Left: Hal Sutton shot to fame in 1983, when at Riviera he won the U.S. P.G.A. Championship by overcoming the mighty Jack Nicklaus during the closing stretch.

possessed the raw talent to progress to the highest level. Faldo's preoccupation for perfection, however, took its toll and he went in search of the master swing, enlisting the help of a then little known teacher, David Leadbetter, and emerged to take on the world and win the majors championships he craved. Faldo might have ruled the world, might have followed in the

Right Larry Nelson with the U.S.
P.G.A. Championship trophy which
he won in 1981 and again in 1987
when he beat Larry Wadkins in a
play-off at P.G.A. National in Florida.

footsteps of Sarazen and Hogan, Player and Nicklaus, all of whom by this time had won all four major championships, if it had not been for Curtis Strange. There are not many players who make successful defenses of major championships, but Strange achieved this at a time when the world was bursting with outstanding golfers. In 1988 he beat Faldo in a play-off at The Country Club, Brookline, Boston, and 12 months later at Oak Hill Country Club, Rochester, New York, Strange outlasted Chip Beck, Mark McCumber, and Ian Woosnam by one shot. He was

Right: Fuzzy Zoeller plays a difficult shot from a greenside bunker during the 1994 U.S.P.G.A. Championship at Southern Hills, Tulsa which was won by Nick Price.

Above: Ray Floyd won the 1976 U.S. Masters, the 1969 and 1982 U.S. P.G.A. Championships and the 1986 U.S. Open.

Left: Bernhard Langer plays from the greenery during the Volvo P.G.A. Championship at Wentworth in 1999 when Colin Montgomerie won for a second successive time.

Above: Nick Faldo with the perfect swing framed by the R & A clubhouse.

Right: Curtis Strange gives the trophy a kiss after winning his second successive U.S. Open title in 1989.

universally considered to be a true champion. Strange, however, would not win another major championship whereas Stewart, a professional since 1979, would not only win the 1989 U.S. P.G.A. Championship and the 1991 U.S. Open but he would also possess the game to return at the end of the decade and capture the 1999 U.S. Open. Stewart was a special golfer, a man possessed with a marvelous talent and a love for mankind, and the family of golf was in mourning when on a fateful day late in 1999 he was killed in a plane crash.

There were others to shine on the 1990s stage. Nick Price, of Zimbabwe, enjoyed two wins in the U.S. P.G.A. Championship and won the Open Championship in 1994 when he edged home from Sweden's Jesper Parnevik. John Daly emerged as the most unlikely winner of a major

championship when at the 1991 U.S. P.G.A. Championship he was called in as ninth and final alternate, driving through the night from his home to reach the Crooked Stick course in Carmel, Indiana, and without so much as the benefit of a practice round he captured the title. Daly also won a play-off against Italy's Costantino Rocca for the 1995 Open Championship at St. Andrews, but distractions off the fairways were to blunt his cutting edge on the straight and narrow.

Tom Lehman, Justin Leonard, and Mark O'Meara all followed Daly as Open Championship winners, O'Meara also winning the Masters in 1998 in which year he was Open champion, before Paul Lawrie became the first Scotsman since Sandy Lyle to win the Open when in 1999 at Carnoustie, where the Championship had not been held since 1975, he

Right: Payne Stewart won the U.S. Open in 1999 at Pinehurst, but he tragically died only months later in an airplane accident.

moved past Jean Van de Velde of France, and Leonard.

Greg Norman was still a force with which to be reckoned. There were many observers who felt that the Australian could move on and secure each of the four major championships as he possessed a superb talent not only to strike the ball with authority but also to adapt his game to all challenges. He did at Royal St. George's in 1993 win the Open Championship for a second time, beating Nick Faldo by two shots, but that was to be his last major championship. Ian Baker-Finch, like Norman from Australia, would also win the Open—his success came at Royal Birkdale in 1991—and compatriots Wayne Grady and Steve Elkington also gleaned major championship honors by virtue of their wins in the 1990 and 1995 U.S. P.G.A. Championships respectively.

Above: Nick Price discusses the technicalities of his game with coach David Leadbetter at the 1999 U.S. Open.

Right: Tom Lehman's victory in the Phoenix Open at the start of 2000 gave him at the age of 40 his fifth U.S. Tour win—his place in the record books has been secured with an Open Championship success in 1996.

Far Right: Justin Leonard completes the traditional trophy kiss at Royal Troon in 1997, where he won the Open Championship ahead of Darren Clarke and Jesper Parnevik.

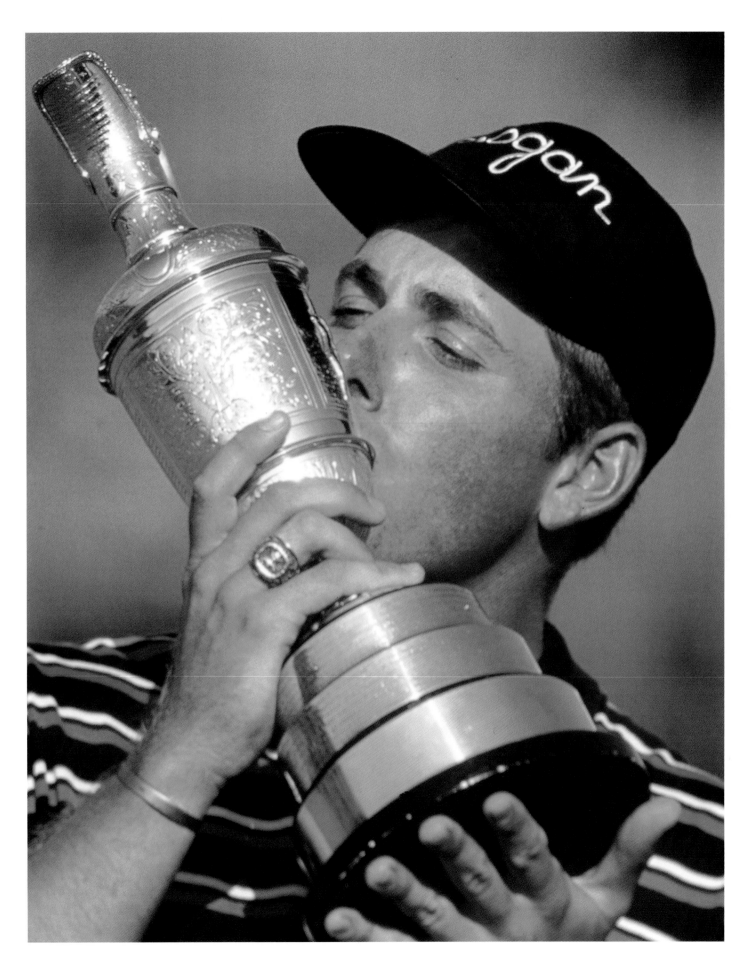

Above: Ernie Els, South Africa's successor to Gary Player and winner of the U.S. Open in both 1994 and 1997.

Spain's José Maria Olazábal, following in the intrepid footsteps of the inspirational Ballesteros, won the Masters Tournament at Augusta National in 1994, and again in 1999, after the Welshman Ian Woosnam (1991) and American Fred Couples (1992) had enjoyed moments to savor in Georgia to where Bernhard Langer (1993) and Ben Crenshaw (1995) returned to win again. Hale Irwin became in 1990, at the age of 45, the oldest winner of the U.S. Open and Tom Kite (1992), Lee Janzen (1993 and 1998), Corey Pavin (1995), and Steve Jones (1996) were among the other Americans to keep their national titles from going overseas.

They were powerless, however, in 1994 and 1997 when Ernie Els, the best South African golfer to emerge since Gary Player, captured the U.S. Open and, on both occasions, pushed into second place Colin Montgomerie, who by now was becoming the dominant golfer on the European Tour. There was a majesty about Montgomerie's golf as he established a record that might never be beaten—unless he continues the run himself—by finishing number one in the European Tour Volvo Order of Merit seven successive times from 1993 to 1999.

So in Europe Montgomerie unquestionably dominated, despite not winning a major championship in the 20th century. However, there can be little doubt that the 1990s were regarded, until the emergence of Tiger Woods, who won the Masters Tournament in 1997 and the U.S. P.G.A.

Left: David Leadbetter coaches Greg Norman at the 1999 Open Championship.

Championship in 1999, as a time when no longer could one man, like Nicklaus, dominate the sport.

By now more and more youngsters were being attracted to golf and honing their games with such swiftness that competition became increasingly keener. Never again would professional golfers finish their rounds and head to the bar; instead the practice grounds became virtually a permanent home for the professionals. There they would eat fruit and swallow bottled water, as they paid more attention to physical fitness and listened to the advice of golfing "gurus"—teachers—with whom they would work diligently, hour after hour, to become better than the next player in the line.

David Leadbetter was one such guru. He looked after Nick Faldo's swing for the best part of 15 years, and if any one player could have dominated the 1990s in Nicklaus-fashion then it was probably Faldo.

In 1985 Faldo, by then a winning force on both sides of the Atlantic but without a major championship to his name, met Leadbetter. By then British-born Leadbetter, who grew up in Zimbabwe playing golf with the likes of Nick Price, Mark McNulty, and Tony Johnstone, had decided that the life of a touring professional was not for him. He had turned to teaching, being offered a club job at Staverton in Northamptonshire, England, and Faldo liked what he heard when they talked.

"There were chinks in my swing which I knew I needed to correct if I wanted to become the player I desired to be and win major championships," said Faldo. "So I decided David was the teacher for me and I asked him to throw the book at me. At times the changes he made me undergo felt weird, really crazy."

Leadbetter admitted: "Nick hung in when others would have dropped out. Come hell or high water, he was determined to get it right. It was a gamble, and he suffered a lot of criticism, but he went all the way down the road. His original swing may have looked beautiful but it would never have stood up to the pressure of winning major championships."

This was the start of a new era in golf as it became increasingly fashionable for players to create their own "team." Faldo had his manager, his teacher, his sponsors, and, in Fanny Sunesson, a loyal caddie who would carry his bag for ten years. Indeed in April, 1990, she became at Augusta National the first women to caddie for a winner in a major championship when Faldo became only the second player in the history of the Masters Tournament to make a successful defense.

Faldo would also win the Open Championship for a second time that year by which time "Team Faldo" was all the rage and Faldo himself was the number one player in the world. He won the Open again in 1992, becoming the first British golfer to win the title three times since Henry Cotton, and the Masters again in 1996. Alongside Ballesteros, Langer, Lyle, and Woosnam, all of whom had been born little more than a year apart, Faldo led a revolution in European golf which, supported by the arrival of Olazábal and Montgomerie, manifested itself in a biennial contest for which the prize was not money but an elegant golden chalice.

Left: Nick Faldo holes the vital putt at the 18th at the 1987 Open Championship at Muirfield.

GOLF'S TICKET TO RIDE

Right: Jack Nicklaus at Muirfield during the 1973 Ryder Cup. It was Nicklaus's instigation that brought European players to the tournament, giving it a new lease of life.

The finest barometer for measuring the balance of power in golf, certainly between Europe and the United States, is the Ryder Cup. In the early days the Ryder Cup was virtually the exclusive property of the United States. The contest was inaugurated in 1927, following two unofficial matches, and the United States and Great Britain gained two wins apiece in the first four encounters of this biennial affair. Subsequently the United States became the dominant force in the game. There was little for Great Britain to cheer about as the British team waited from 1933 to 1957 for another win. That year Dai Rees led them to victory at Lindrick.

Thereafter the United States resumed command. America continued to win with consummate ease, except for a tie at Royal Birkdale in 1969, and it was feared in some quarters that the contest would become extinct unless it was revitalized. It was Jack Nicklaus who approached Lord Derby, the President of the British P.G.A., with the suggestion that the inclusion of players from the continent of Europe might foster a new beginning for the match. Nicklaus did not want the Ryder Cup to die and he was concerned that it might. Consequently the British P.G.A. convened a special committee meeting at which it was decided to vary the Deed of Trust, with the result that Nicklaus's suggestion was sanctioned.

Initially, it did not appear to make a scrap of difference. Severiano Ballesteros and Antonio Garrido, both of Spain, were included in the European team in 1979 but they lost heavily by 17-11 at The Greenbrier in West Virginia. There was to be an even more humiliating reversal for the Europeans two years later when on home territory at Walton Heath in Surrey they went down 18-9. The United States sent over 12 outstanding players to participate in the contest, and romped to victory.

The team consisted of Jack Nicklaus, Tom Watson, Lee Trevino, Ray Floyd, Johnny Miller, Tom Kite, Ben Crenshaw, Hale Irwin, Jerry Pate, Bill Rogers, Bruce Leitzke, and Larry Nelson. The European team, with Seve Ballesteros absent and Tony Jacklin also excluded for the first time since 1967, did not have the winner of a major championship in their squad. It was like taking lambs to the slaughter.

Yet there was a growing sense of achievement in Europe. Ballesteros, in spite of his confrontations with officialdom, had matured into the finest player in the world. He did not, of course, possess the record of Nicklaus but he could, on the day, take on any player with the belief that he was the favorite to win. By dint of his record in the United States and around the world, he set an example for his European colleagues.

Thus with Ballesteros's encouragement and the inspiration of Jacklin, now the captain, Europe came within a whisker of winning the 1983 contest at the P.G.A. National Golf Club at Palm

Above: The Ryder Cup trophy.

Right: Action at the 1985 Ryder Cup at The Belfry in Sutton Coldfield, England, where Europe gave the American team their first defeat since 1957.

Beach Gardens, Florida. There, with Nicklaus in charge, the United States squeezed home by 14½-13½.

There was cause to celebrate as far as Europe was concerned, because this result unquestionably raised the possibility of victory being attained at The Belfry, Sutton Coldfield, in 1985. By now Ballesteros was the winner of four major championships and during 1985 Bernhard Langer had won the U.S. Masters while Sandy Lyle had become the first British player since Jacklin in 1969 to win the Open Championship.

With Jacklin once more at the helm there was such confidence in the European camp that the American team, led on this occasion by Lee Trevino, suffered a shattering blow to their pride when they were beaten 16½-11½. There were

now four Spaniards in the team—Ballesteros, Jose-Maria Canizares, Pinero, and Jose Rivero—and little Pinero exemplified the determination among the Europeans by leading off in the singles to beat Lanny Wadkins.

Many observers of this exciting game were in agreement at the time that the match swung on a putt of little more than 15 inches that Craig Stadler had missed on the last green in the four-balls on the second morning. That cost the Americans the lead which they would never regain. In retrospect, Stadler's alarming miss might be regarded as the moment when the pendulum swung. Most certainly it lit the blue touchpaper on another explosive boom, with the European Tour growing in strength as an increasing number of sponsors, especially on the

Right: Craig Stadler of the U.S.A. misses a vital putt on the 18th during the 1985 Ryder Cup at the Belfry.

continent, stampeded their way onto the scene.

With the onrush of money—the Tour's over-all purse multiplied nearly tenfold between 1980 and 1988—came a new breed of player. Suddenly the practice grounds of Europe were frequented like those in the United States. More golfers from other countries, especially Australia, joined the circuit, and this helped to heighten competition. Countries on the European continent were also

producing more golfers. For instance, in Sweden there had begun one of the most disciplined training programs in the history of sport. Jan Blomquist had been charged with raising the standing of golf to such a degree that Sweden could be as proud of their golfers as they were of their tennis players such as Bjorn Borg.

In 1980 Blomquist took a team of Swedes to the Eisenhower Trophy, the world amateur team

Above: The European Team celebrate their historic 1987 Ryder Cup victory at Muirfield Village with captain Tony Jacklin holding the Cup.

Right: America's Craig Stadler.

Left: Ove Sellberg, who in 1986 became the first Swedish player to win on the European Tour when he captured the Epson Grand Prix of Europe.

Right: Sweden's Mats Lanner took the
baton from Ove Sellberg to win the
same event the following year.

championship, and they were palpably outclassed. The United States won, with Sweden trailing home eighth, more than 40 strokes behind. Blomquist stuck to his guns and he implemented a training program that included a strict diet, no alcohol, weight-training, and psychological talks. In 1982 Sweden finished second to the United States in the Eisenhower Trophy and Ove Sellberg, a member of that team, became in 1986 the first Swedish player to win on the European

Tour. He won the Epson Grand Prix, a match-play event, at the St. Pierre Country Club, Chepstow, and 12 months later his successor was his compatriot Mats Lanner.

Jacklin had predicted following the Ryder Cup match at The Belfry in 1985 that the next European team would contain a Swedish player. However, although Anders Forsbrand, another Swedish player, won the European Masters at Crans-sur-Sierre, Switzerland, he was too late to earn a place in the 1987 team. Jacklin's prophecy would, nevertheless, come true as in successive contests Joakim Haeggman (1993), Per-Ulrik Johansson (1995), and Jesper Parnevik (1997) all made the team. Denmark's Thomas Bjorn also joined in 1997, and then in 1999 both Jarmo Sandelin and Parnevik, who by now was enjoying success on the U.S. Tour as well as the European Tour, played.

In 1987 the European team produced the most telling and satisfying result in the history of the competition. A team of four Scotsmen, three Spaniards, two Englishmen, one Irishman, one Welshman, and one German linked together to win on American soil for the first time. The score of 15-13 is a minor consideration. For Tony Jacklin and Jack Nicklaus, the respective European and American captains, it was a watershed in the game.

Jacklin and Nicklaus voiced their agreement following the end of the match that Europe's success could change the face of world golf. Nicklaus had announced prior to the match that he felt that his team as a whole had great strength and that the European team was still very much the underdog. He clearly considered the American team to have a supreme advantage with the match being contested on the course that he had built at Muirfield Village.

In one sense, possibly through the internationalization of golf, it appeared that playing at home was no longer a great advantage. The

Above: Paul Way (left), Sam Torrance (center), and Ian Woosnam celebrate the European win at the 1985 Ryder Cup.

Right: Tom Lehman of the U.S.A.
celebrates a birdie at the 33rd
Ryder Cup in 1999.

emerging new stars traveled easily, and increasingly more comfortably, and possessed the armory to take on any challenge.

The Americans, of course, had long since proved that they could adapt their games, more suited to the receptive greens found on their home circuit, to challenge for major honors on the links where each year the Open Championship unfolded. Now the world's brightest players were prepared to venture more frequently into the Americans' backyard, and show that they were equally impressive at taking on their rivals at their own game.

The Ryder Cup, following Europe's successive wins in 1985 and 1987, had very much sprung to life with capacity crowds on both sides of the Atlantic and in 1989 at The Belfry the two teams proved inseparable as they tied 14-14. It was only the second time in the history of the match that

the two teams had shared the spoils, albeit that Europe retained the Cup as the holders, and the contest captured the attention and earned the admiration of millions of people around the world with a script that twisted and turned through three days of high-octane excitement.

As Tony Jacklin, once again the captain of Europe, observed: "What was so important was that the game of golf was richer for what happened at The Belfry as Europe held onto the Cup and the Americans restored their pride."

Ray Floyd, the U.S. captain, said: "There were a lot of peaks and valleys. Early on I felt like a tie was a defeat. Later on I thought we had no chance at all. To come back after that and draw tickles me to death. Golf has been the winner."

Europe had led 14-10, but the Americans won the last four matches on the Brabazon course. Two years later at Kiawah Island in South

Carolina the Americans maintained their momentum, leading 3-1 after the first morning foursomes, but, typically, the Europeans fought back so that by winning the fourballs on the afternoon of the second day the teams entered the final series of 12 singles locked together at 8-8. There was controversy when Steve Pate, who had played the previous afternoon, withdrew from the singles through injury, and the tension of that last day reached its climax when Bernhard Langer faced a putt of six feet on the last green against Hale Irwin. If Langer holed then the match would be drawn again, and Europe would retain the Cup. Bernard Gallacher was now Europe's captain but his predecessor, Jacklin, would say as Langer crouched over his putt that "no man should have to bear such pressure." Michael Bonallack, then the secretary of the Royal and Ancient, would call it: "The greatest pressure putt in the history of golf."

It is now history that Langer missed, and the Americans won 14½ to 13½, but there was a wonderful moment for the German golfer, of whom no praise is too high, when only one week later he captured the German Masters. Langer's resilience had never been questioned and his sheer determination has, perhaps, never been more evident than that week back home in his own country when he was fighting a temperature of 102 and playing against his doctor's advice. He holed from 12 feet at the last to tie the Australian Rodger Davis, and won the play-off at the first extra hole.

In 1993 the Ryder Cup returned for a third time to The Belfry. Europe initially held the advantage, taking with them a one point lead into the singles, but on this occasion the Americans found strength in the "middle order" and

prevailed 15-13. Gallacher remained at the helm for a third successive match but Europe traveled to Oak Hill Country Club in Rochester, New York, as the underdogs.

It appeared that the American golfers might be on the threshold of dominating the sport again. For the first time since 1986 no European had won a major championship and Lanny Wadkins, the United States captain, felt supremely confident with his team. Wadkins slept well, too, following the first two days of foursomes and fourballs, with the Americans 9-7 in front, but Gallacher was convinced as he sipped only half a glass of beer that evening that his team could respond to the challenge.

They did not let him down. First Howard Clark and Mark James won, then Ian Woosnam halved with Fred Couples and after David Gilford, Colin Montgomerie, Nick Faldo, with a remarkable recovery against Curtis Strange, and Sam Torrance had all gained hard-earned victories on the 17th and 18th greens so Philip Walton came to the last hole where he outstayed Jay Haas to secure a famous triumph. It was only the second time that Europe had won the Ryder Cup on American soil.

Now the Ryder Cup moved to new territory as, for the first time, the match was played on the continent and, appropriately, in Spain where Ballesteros, the inspiration behind Europe's revival, was captain.

There had never been a match quite like this one, and there probably never will be. The European team comprising one Dane, two Englishmen, one German, one Irishman, one Italian, one Scotsman, two Swedes, two Spaniards, and a Welshman, were galvanized by Ballesteros. They led 10½-5½ going into the singles. Tom Kite,

Right: Lanny Wadkins, captain of the
1995 American Ryder Cup team,
had to watch Europe walk away
with the trophy on American soil as
Bernard Gallacher superbly led his
team to a famous triumph.

the American captain, was hopeful, if nothing more, that his team could fight back. They did, with some style, as Fred Couples handed out an 8 and 7 mauling to Ian Woosnam in the opening singles and, if it had not been for Per-Ulrik Johansson and Costantino Rocca gaining vital wins against Davis Love III and Tiger Woods respectively in the next two matches on the course then the result quite probably would have been different. The Europeans, however, had the dependable Bernhard Langer, who beat Brad Faxon, to rely upon, and when Colin Montgomerie halved with Scott Hoch they had retained the Cup by 14½-13½.

The last Ryder Cup of the 20th century would unfold at The Country Club, Brookline, on the outskirts of Boston. It was an appropriate setting. The Country Club, founded in 1882, is one of the world's most renowned golf venues and lies just 45 miles from Worcester, Massachusetts, where the inaugural Ryder Cup match was staged in 1927. This time the

Americans had only one rookie on their team—David Duval, who at the time was second in the Official World Golf Ranking to Woods. Europe had seven rookies—Paul Lawrie, the new Open Champion, Sergio Garcia, Jean Van de Velde, the first Frenchman to play in the match, Jarmo Sandelin, Miguel Angel Jiménez, Padraig Harrington, and Andrew Coltart—and in Mark James a new captain.

There were a number of notable absentees with Ballesteros, Faldo, Langer, Lyle, and Woosnam all collectively missing for the first time since the players from the continent of Europe became eligible for the match in 1979.

Ben Crenshaw, the American captain, was confident that his team would win and improve their recent record as Europe had won four times and tied once in the seven matches since 1985.

Crenshaw's confidence soon subsided. For the first two days Europe's so-called underdogs produced one outstanding performance after

Above: Justin Leonard was a member of the U.S. Team which regained the Ryder Cup in 1999.

Right: Hal Sutton in a jubilant mood
at the 1999 Ryder Cup.

another with a combination of sparkling golf, sheer guts, and smart captaincy. James, supported by assistant captains Ken Brown and Sam Torrance, who was to be named captain for the 2001 match, refused to be deflected from his determination to build a substantial lead and he kept faith throughout the foursomes and four-balls with pre-determined partnerships.

His players supported him with such style, with Jesper Parnevik and Garcia forming an unbeatable partnership, that on entering the singles Europe required only four points from 12 matches to secure a third successive Ryder Cup win.

The final day would be remembered for an invasion of the 17th green, when Justin Leonard holed a huge putt against José Maria Olazábal to complete a remarkable recovery by the Americans, because at that moment the game's high sporting values were seriously questioned by those who observe the sport. Nevertheless, the Americans could point to them winning each of the first six singles with world class perform-ances that transformed the situation and event-ually left Crenshaw holding Samuel Ryder's Cup.

Europe's brave bid had been thwarted, and with seven newcomers in the team it provided ample evidence that as a new millennium dawned so the fairways of the world would be graced by new faces eager to take on the challenge now being set by a young golfer who was picking up the record books and ripping them to shreds.

TIGER—AND THE SUPERSTARS OF THE NEW MILLENNIUM

Right: Tiger Woods at the World Golf Championships—N.E.C. Invitational which he won by one stroke from Phil Mickelson at Firestone C.C., Akron, Ohio.

No player strode more purposely into the new millennium than Tiger Woods. For many years the emerging professionals had implied with both deeds and words that never again would one player dominate the sport as Jack Nicklaus had done, and most observers of the game formed a similar opinion.

Then along came Woods to blow smoke in the faces of everyone. There were those, of course, who instantly recognized in Woods a gifted individual. After all, at the age of two, he displayed his precocious talent on coast-to-coast television when he putted against Bob Hope on the Mike Douglas Show. Nicknamed "Tiger," after a Vietnamese soldier who was a friend of his father, he had shot 48 for nine holes at the age of three and featured in the American magazine *Golf Digest* at the age of five.

Woods himself maintains that his love affair with golf began before he could walk or talk. His father, Earl, was an accomplished golfer and in his book, *Training a Tiger*, his son pointed out:

"I don't remember sitting in my high chair in the garage watching Pop hit balls. But what I do remember is an early fascination with the game because Pop seemed to enjoy it so much. In retrospect, golf for me was an apparent attempt to emulate the person I looked up to more than anyone: my father.

"He says I was unusually attentive for my age. I was also very eager to learn as much as I could

about the game that had so thoroughly captivated my father. I remember a daily ritual we had when I was a child: I would call Pop at work to ask if I could practice with him. He would always pause for a second or two—keeping me in suspense—but he always said yes. Then Mom would drop me off at the golf course to meet Pop for practice. In his own way he was teaching me initiative. You see, he never pushed me to play. Whether I practiced or played was always my idea. He was instrumental in helping me develop the drive to achieve, but his role—as well as my mother's—was one of support and guidance, not interference, well-meaning or otherwise."

That drive to achieve, coupled with an innate talent to play the game, would see Tiger Woods develop into a colossal superstar. Born on December 30, 1975, he progressed to win the U.S. Junior Amateur in 1991, 1992, and 1993. Then in 1994 he became the youngest winner of the U.S. Amateur Championship which he successfully defended twice and in so doing became the first golfer to win that title three years in succession.

Just about his only disappointment in a scintillating amateur career came at Royal Porthcawl in Wales when he was on the losing United States team in the Walker Cup. Yet in six major championships as an amateur he survived the halfway cut on four occasions and in 1995 he was the low amateur in both the Masters Tournament at Augusta National and the U.S.

Far Left: Woods at the Johnnie Walker Classic in 1999.

Left: The National Car Rental Golf Classic on the Magnolia golf course, Disney World.

Below Left: A reflective portrait of golf's biggest star of the new millennium— Tiger Woods.

Right: Tiger on the fairway at the

Firestone Country Club, Akron,

Ohio.

Open at Shinnecock Hills. There was by now no questioning the quality of his play, his desire, or his dedication.

Eldrick "Tiger" Woods had taken his huge reputation to Augusta and he responded by out-hitting the likes of Fred Couples and Greg Norman in practice. Jack Nicklaus cooed: "I had no idea how long he was!" His iron play let him down that week, but he would conquer Augusta only two years later.

In fact Woods made his professional debut, to a fanfare of high expectations, in the Greater Milwaukee Open at Brown Deer Park on August 29, 1996. He opened with a 67, and compiled two other sub-70 scores, but on a low scoring course he finished tied 60th behind Loren Roberts.

It was only the start. Woods played in eight U.S. P.G.A. Tour events in 1996. He won twice, registered three other top ten finishes and apart from his debut at Milwaukee he did not finish out of the leading 25 in any tournament. He earned $790,594 and received the Rookie of the Year Award. Woods recorded his first U.S. Tour win on October 6, in the Las Vegas Invitational when he came from four behind the leader with a last round of 64 to tie with Davis Love III and won the play-off at the first extra hole. He was third the following week and, one week later, triumphed again in the Walt Disney World/Oldsmobile Golf Classic.

There had never seemed to be any doubt about it, of course, but with those two wins in three weeks a star was born. If there were any doubting Thomases then they were compelled to accept that Tiger Woods was indeed a genius when he annihilated the field at the 61st Masters Tournament in 1997. He won by a record 12 shots despite playing the first nine holes in 40.

It was the worst start by a champion and one of 18 Masters records that he would set over those four tumultuous days at Augusta National.

Tournament historian Bill Inglish recorded that Woods achieved:

Low 72-hole total of 270 (70-66-65-69), 18 under par

Youngest champion at the age of 21

The widest margin of victory—12 shots

Low score for last 54 holes—200 (16 under par)

Largest lead for first 54-holes—nine shots

Youngest leader for first 54-holes—Age 21

Low score for middle 36 holes—131 (66-65)

Youngest leader for first 36-holes—Age 21

Most shots under par for second nine—16 (30-32-33-33)

Second nine in pars or better—2 eagles, 12 birdies, 22 pars

Most shots under par final 63 holes—22

Worst start by champion first nine holes—40

Champion in first professional start as a participant

Most threes by champion—26 (14 birdies, two eagles, ten pars)

Youngest participant to score 65—Age 21

Youngest participant to score 66—Age 21

Youngest participant to score 30 on second nine— Age 21

19 under par in 45 holes span beginning with tenth hole (30-66-65)

In 1975 Lee Elder had become the first black golfer to be invited to play in the Masters. Now at the age of 21 years, three months, and 14 days (Severiano Ballesteros was 23 years and four days old when he won in 1980) Woods had become the first person of color to win the Masters.

He would not, however, go in the record books as the youngest winner of a major cham-

pionship. Those honors still belonged to John McDermott, who won the U.S. Open in 1911 at 19 years, ten months, and 14 days. "Young" Tom Morris, who won the Open Championship in 1868 at 17 years, five months, and eight days, and Gene Sarazen, who won the U.S. P.G.A. Championship in 1922 at 20 years, five months, and 22 days.

Nevertheless the Tiger Woods era had begun. As Jack Nicklaus observed: "I don't think we've had a whole lot happen in, well, ten years. Some guys, yes, have come along and won tournaments but no one player has sustained and dominated. I think we might have somebody now."

Most certainly the timing could not have been better as far as the U.S. P.G.A. Tour was concerned. It was reported that the emergence of Woods had provided the springboard for Tim Finchem, the Commissioner of the P.G.A. Tour, to conclude new television contracts in the May of 1997, and which would take effect in 1999, to increase annual coverage from 350 hours to more than 400 hours and provide gross revenues

of $400 million through 2002 which more than doubled the previous package.

Finchem projected that official prize money would grow from $78 million in 1997 to more than $93 million in 1998 and escalate to more than $150 million by 2002. The average prize money per event was projected to increase from $1.7 million in 1997 to more than $3 million in 2000 and $3.5 million in 2002.

In fact Finchem was able to announce that for the millennium season players on the P.G.A. Tour would compete for approximately $157 million in official prize money and that virtually every round would be televised.

Woods, with three other wins, was ranked number one on the U.S. Tour money list in 1997, but his star did not burn so brightly in 1998 when he slipped to fourth place in the annual rankings with only the one win in the Bell South Classic. He did not finish outside of the top 20 in any of the four major championships, with a best finish of third in the Open Championship, but the golfing world was to learn in 1999 why this was the case. Woods explained:

"I had to make a change in my technique. If you look at the tapes of my swing in 1997, and study the club position, then you can see it was across the line and it was shut. I had trouble controlling my distances. I also wasn't as good a wedge player as I wanted to be. I figured I needed to change a few things—in fact I changed a lot. But what I learned most was to try to control the club at impact a little better by controlling the speed. I learned to swing the club through a different plane, and shape the golf ball the way I wanted to do."

Some days Woods had hit up to 800 balls on the range to hone that swing. The work ethics of professional golfers had long since changed, but Woods was now displaying a determination that was beyond anything that anyone in the game had ever witnessed. He claimed he had been winning without his "A" game, and in 1999 Woods supplied all the evidence that his work regime on the practice range, where he is tutored by Butch Harmon, had provided him with the ammunition to attack the record books.

Woods was 16 years old when first Harmon worked with him on the range. Since then they have been inseparable. Harmon is also an analyst for Sky Television and their viewers have been privileged to receive almost weekly updates on the refinements that Woods habitually makes to his swing as he constantly seeks to improve.

There is no question that Harmon is in awe of the Woods talent, and rightly so, but there is a special bond between them built out of mutual respect. Harmon said: "Tiger is totally dedicated to being the best player in the world and he has got the talent to do it. The great thing about Tiger is his attitude. People talk about the importance of the mental side of golf and he is very strong mentally. His mind is very well controlled and he is always in control of himself on the golf course."

There were those who suggested that this might not be the case in 1998, but there can be no doubt that this was the year when Woods strengthened his game and his resolve and laid the foundations to enter the new millennium as the man to beat. "The great thing is that Tiger is a wonderful student," said Harmon. "He is a sponge, he soaks up everything you tell him. His desire to learn is beyond belief, which is why I try to teach him difficult shots. I have worked with him over the years adapting his swing as he moved from a teenager to an adult and grown in body and strength. The difficult part for me is making sure that I am right in what I tell him—the changes I make. Then again I have worked with Darren Clarke, Davis Love III, and Greg Norman and, with due respect to them all, none of them has such God-given talent as Tiger. He has so much talent he can do anything on the golf course."

These words would ring in the ears of Wood's rivals throughout 1999. He returned to number one on the U.S. P.G.A. Tour money list with eight victories pushing his official earnings to $6,616,585 alone. The growth in prize money had been dramatic, but nothing emphasized it more than the statistic that those winnings outstripped by almost $1,000,000 the sum that Nicklaus, buoyed by 70 U.S. P.G.A. titles and 18 professional majors, had won in his entire career. In 1999 Woods also found major championship glory again, winning the U.S. P.G.A. Championship at Medinah Country Club, and he collected for good measure two of the recently introduced World Golf Championships which were the

Left: Davis Love III at the P.G.A.

Grand Slam of Golf in Hawaii, 1999.

result of the tours coming together through the International Federation of P.G.A. Tours to further enhance the internationalization of the game.

For good measure Woods also won on the European Tour, capturing the Deutsche Bank—S.A.P. Open T.P.C. of Europe, and in partnership with American compatriot Mark O'Meara regained for the United States the World Cup of Golf in which he was also the individual winner.

In short he was setting new standards, and attracting more and more people to the game, as his achievements guaranteed more publicity for golf. When he won the Mercedes Championships in January, 2000, it gave him his eighth victory in his last 11 U.S. P.G.A. Tour events and his fifth in a row. Those five in a row represented the longest winning streak on the U.S. P.G.A. Tour since Ben Hogan in 1948. In fact there were those that argued that, given the increasing strength of competition, his sequence could be compared with the 11 tournament winning run made by Byron Nelson in 1945.

Ernie Els, whom Woods beat in a play-off for the Mercedes Championship, said: "He's a legend in the making if he isn't one already. He's only 24, so he'll probably be bigger than Elvis when he gets to 40."

The legend continued to grow as Woods, increasing in maturity and apparently well able to cope with difficult situations, came from seven behind with eight holes to play to overhaul Matt Gogel and win the Pebble Beach National Pro-Am. He closed with a 64, finishing four under for the last four holes, to take his winnings from six events to $4,592,000 compared with the $63,355 worth of war bonds Nelson won for his 11 events! Nelson, who at the age of 88 watched the

Woods performance of television, said: "You have to be amazed by Tiger. I get more publicity now because of Tiger Woods than I got the whole time back then."

The Woods publicity machine was not only boosting Tiger's bank balance, through lucrative endorsements, but also heightening golf's following. The next week at the Buick International it was reported that the two mile stretch of road from Interstate Highway 5 in San Diego to Torrey Pines golf course was bumper to bumper 30 minutes before Woods teed off. Ticket sales were astronomical and Phil Mickelson, one of a number of players whom it was felt might make it to number one in the world prior to the arrival of Woods, said: "The way Tiger has played the last six events, and prior to that, has generated a lot of interest in the game. The galleries are so large this week that they couldn't accommodate it parking-wise…and I'm a beneficiary of that. I'm making more money because Tiger is helping to increase the prize funds. He is creating more excitement in the game of golf. All the players are beneficiaries."

Woods did not win at San Diego so his six-in-a-row stretch, which equalled the number set by Ben Hogan in 1948, came to an end. Although little more than one month later he registered his 18th U.S. Tour win by collecting the Bay Hill Invitational title and received the prize from Arnold Palmer. At such a tender age he was already being compared with great sportsmen from other sports, such as the N.H.L.'s Wayne Gretzky and N.B.A.'s Michael Jordan, and, of course, in golf the question that was being asked was: "Who would challenge Tiger as the years unfolded?"

In truth the game was rich in talent. Sadly

Payne Stewart, winner of the U.S. Open in 1999, had died in a plane crash later that year but American contemporaries such as Davis Love III, Fred Couples, Jim Furyk, Lee Janzen, Tom Lehman, Phil Mickelson, Mark O'Meara, and Hal Sutton were still rivals for Woods in addition to England's Nick Faldo, Germany's Bernhard Langer, Zimbabwe's Nick Price, Fiji's Vijay Singh, Spain's José Maria Olazábal, Australia's Greg Norman and Steve Elkington, South Africa's Ernie Els and Ian Woosnan of Wales.

These were all experienced players, many of whom had been touted at one time or another to become the number one player in the world or indeed had reached such exalted status, but with the dawning of the new millennium so the spotlight began to focus on a new group of inspirational young players.

David Duval and Justin Leonard were, perhaps, the best known of the younger Americans to have emerged as serious American challengers although such was the progress of the game on an international front that in Sergio Garcia it appeared that Spain had a worthy successor to

Seve Ballesteros and José Maria Olazábal. Aaron Baddeley was seen as the next Greg Norman to come out of Australia, Retief Goosen and Hennie Otto seemed poised to follow in the footsteps of South African compatriots Bobby Locke, Gary Player and Ernie Els and Carlos Franco (Paraguay), Stuart Appleby (Australia), Mike Weir (Canada), Shigeki Maruyama (Japan), Michael Campbell (New Zealand), and Angel Cabrera (Argentina) were others to be on the threshold of greatness.

Moreover in Europe there were a plethora of challengers led by Colin Montgomerie (Scotland), Lee Westwood (England), Jesper Parnevik (Sweden), Darren Clarke (Northern Ireland), Miguel Angel Jiménez (Spain), Thomas Bjorn (Denmark), Paul Lawrie (Scotland), Robert Karlsson (Sweden), Padraig Harrington (Ireland), Jarmo Sandelin (Sweden), Andrew Coltart (Scotland), Phillip Price (Wales), Jean Van de Velde (France), Patrik Sjoland (Sweden), and Per-Ulrik Johansson (Sweden).

This, then, was the brave new world of the 21st century. The birth of the International

Right: Justin Leonard at the Tour

Championship, Houston, Texas, in

1999.

Federation of P.G.A. Tours in 1996 would bring together the Tours of Asia, Australia, Europe, Japan, South Africa, and the United States to ensure that the game built on a foundation of integrity would progress in an orderly and structured fashion. Greg Norman had initially proposed a world tour because the leading players held a strong desire to examine their games more regularly against their peers on the international stage.

In its original concept such a world tour would have competed directly with the Tours themselves and Tim Finchem and Ken Schofield, the Commissioner of the U.S. P.G.A. Tour and the Executive Director of the European Tour respectively, provided a blueprint for Norman's proposals to move forward without harming the future of the sport.

In 1999 the World Golf Championships were born when for the first time the Andersen Consulting Match Play, the N.E.C. Invitational, and the American Express Championship were played and in 2000 a fourth event was added when the W.G.C.—E.M.C. World Cup, first played as the Canada Cup in 1953, came under the umbrella of the International Federation of P.G.A. Tours and was scheduled to be played at Buenos Aires Golf Club in Argentina. The international arena had already benefited when in 1994 The Presidents Cup Match was developed to give the world's best non-European players an opportunity to compete in international team match-play competition—the United States won in 1994 and 1996 before the International Team triumphed in 1998—and in 2000 another biennial match began with the Eurobet Seve Ballesteros Trophy featuring a team from Continental Europe against one from Great Britain and Ireland. Seve Ballesteros

led Continental Europe to victory at Sunningdale.

Now the best of the world would not only pit themselves against each other in the famous major championships, and the Ryder Cup, but also in the World Golf Championships, the Presidents Cup, and the Seve Ballesteros Trophy. Most certainly the arrival of the World Golf Championships provided additional opportunities for players to elevate themselves in the Official World Golf Ranking, which is endorsed by the organizations that conduct the four major championships and the six professional tours that make up the International Federation of P.G.A. Tours. This ranking list is issued every Monday following the completion of the previous week's tournaments from around the world. The results are evaluated and points are awarded according to the finishing positions of the players with the points for each player accumulating over a two-year "rolling" period, with the points awarded in the most recent 52-week period doubled. It was hardly a surprise, given the manner in which he was invading the record books, that Tiger Woods had built a substantial lead as the year 2000 began to unfold.

The World Golf Championships had certainly provided a compelling new series to assist the progress of the professional game. Schofield pointed out: "Greg Norman's ideas brought the possibility of additional world events to the forefront, putting them more in focus. The key was the timing. Deane Beman had had a very long and superb run at the helm of the U.S. P.G.A. Tour, making them what they are. But for this to happen so early in Tom Finchem's reign gave them the impetus to realize there was a broader horizon than simply having a tour within the States. It proved they could work with us and

Right: Davis Love III, ranked among the top four players in the world at the beginning of 2000.

Below Right: Phil Mickelson of the U.S.A. at the Mercedes Championship in 1999. Victories in the Buick Invitational, the Bell South Classic and the MasterCard Colonial in the first five months of 2000 took his total of U.S. tour victories to 16.

others to play their part in the world game. It probably came more natural for ourselves given the co-operation we have had with southern hemisphere Tours. For us, it was a natural progression of how the game was moving internationally."

Indeed the 2000 European Tour International Schedule, a new title reflecting no fewer than 35 host nations, provided abundant evidence of the European Tour's determination to internationalize the game of golf whilst maintaining a policy of opportunity and incentive. A record total of 43 tournaments through 22 countries was announced for the 2000 Volvo Order of Merit, with substantial increases in prize money, and in total it was announced that the European Tour, the European Seniors Tour, and the European Challenge Tour would visit an unprecedented 35 countries.

The European Tour had since its birth in October, 1971, been at the forefront of recogniz-

ing that golf is an international game and that geographical boundaries should not be allowed to stifle progress. So came the creation of an early season schedule with co-sanctioned events involving the Tours of Asia, Australia, Europe, and South Africa. Prize money had also risen from £427,917 in 1975 to more than £50,000,000 on the European Tour in 2000.

In America the growth of the P.G.A. TOUR, the Senior P.G.A. Tour and the Buy.Com Tour was reflected in the purses which, supported by revenue from television income, rose from $6,000,000 in 1970 to $46,000,000 in 1990 and $157,000,000 in 2000. Finchem pointed out that that the schedule had been revised and "segmented" to allow for "greater promotion of our events by our network broadcast partners."

The Seniors P.G.A. Tour, replicated in Europe during the last decade of the 20th century, sprang from discussions in late 1978 and 1979 in which leading senior players expressed interest in playing several "senior" events. Its phenomenal growth was reflected by the achievement in 1997 of Hale Irwin, who became the first player on any tour to surpass $2,000,000 in prize money in a single season.

In 1999 Bruce Fleisher raised the stakes still further by earning $2,515,705 and, with Jack Nicklaus celebrating his 60th birthday on January 21, 2000, so the signs were that the Seniors Tour would continue to progress and the Buy.Com Tour and the European Challenge Tour would continue to mature the stars of tomorrow.

Nicklaus, however, was among those at the forefront of the sport to emphasize that by now the focus was on Woods and his young rivals. In America David Duval was seen as the main competitor to Woods and, indeed, he had enjoyed a spell as number one in the world. Born

and raised in Florida, and the son of Bob Duval, a winner on the P.G.A. Seniors Tour, he grew up playing at Timiquana Country Club where his father was the professional. In keeping with so many of the leading American golfers of today, he came through the American college system, studying at Georgia Tech in Atlanta.

In 1991 Duval was a member of the victorious United States Walker Cup team. He served his professional apprenticeship on the Nike Tour, which in 2000 became the Buy.Com Tour and is the equivalent of the European Challenge Tour, and in his first full year on the U.S. Tour in 1995 he finished 11th in the money list.

Duval climbed to tenth place the next year but, as in 1995, he failed to win. Some observers initially felt that Duval might develop into a good journeyman professional, especially as he was runner-up on no fewer than seven occasions, but all that changed after he closed the 1997 season with three victories. In 1998 he won four times to climb to number one in the money list and, although overshadowed by Woods in 1999 despite scoring a final round of 59 to win the Bob Hope Chrsyler Classic in addition to capturing three other titles, he entered the year 2000 in second place in the Official World Golf Ranking.

Duval is essentially a private person, one who shuns high profile publicity, and albeit that he wears sunglasses because his eyes are overly sensitive to light, they seem to reflect his personality. "I'm not comfortable with fame," he said. "I don't think the golfing public or the writers have a right to know everything about me. If that seems stand-offish then I apologize. I simply don't find it necessary to reveal every detail. Everybody wants me to talk about what happened to my brother (he died in spite of

Right: Carlos Franco of Paraguay won twice on the U.S. Tour in 1999 when he was Rookie of the Year, and he is seen here representing his country in the Alfred Dunhill Cup at St Andrews. In 2000 he made a successful defense of the Compaq Classic of New Orleans.

receiving a bone marrow transplant from David). I don't want to talk about it."

What Duval does is to talk with his clubs. He always appears unflappable on the course and even when he completed that 59 he did little more than simply smile. He did enjoy, however, his debut in the Ryder Cup in 1999 when he beat Jesper Parnevik five and four in the singles and he likes nothing more than a challenge. No other player in America, apart from Woods, produced a finer record at the end of the 20th century than Duval and he was well aware that to maintain momentum he would be required to graduate to winning a major championship.

Justin Leonard put such obstacles behind him in winning the Open Championship at Royal Troon in 1997, when Darren Clarke and Jesper Parnevik were runners-up, and he came within a whisker of regaining the title at Carnoustie in 1999 when Paul Lawrie won the three-man play-off. When Leonard, who learned his trade on courses in and around Dallas, Texas, where he was brought up, joined the U.S. P.G.A. Tour in 1994 he had already played in eight Tour events

as an amateur and made the cut on no fewer than five occasions. He earned his Tour privileges without needing to go to the Qualifying School, as he finished third in the 1994 Anheuser-Busch Classic, on only his third start as a professional. His first success soon followed in the 1996 Buick Classic. Like Duval, he came into the new millennium with his 30th birthday ahead of him and in contrast Davis Love III, aged 36 at the time of the 2000 Masters Tournament, can be considered a veteran.

Even so Love was ranked among the top four in the world when the 2000 season began and, like Phil Mickelson, aged 30, he was regarded as a player with the armory to take on Woods. There was good reason for this because Love had won no fewer than 13 U.S. Tour titles, including the U.S. P.G.A. Championship in 1997. Love was a three-time all-American at North Carolina and won the 1984 North and South Amateur and he had informed his father, Davis Love, Jnr., a former touring professional, at the age of nine that he wanted to play golf for a living. He turned professional in 1985 with the reputation of being

capable of hitting the ball awesome distances, and by 1987 he had won the M.C.I. Heritage Classic. His father was sadly killed in a plane crash the following year, but he had by then taught his son to master the golf swing as well as to understand the game's lore.

In 1991 Mickelson became the first amateur since 1985 to win on the U.S. Tour when he captured the Northern Telecom Open. He turned professional the following year and took his number of victories on the U.S. P.G.A. Tour to 16 with his successes in the 2000 Buick International, the Bell South Classic and the MasterCard Colonial. Mickelson, who played on two United States Walker Cup teams, has progressed to be regarded as the best left-handed golfer in the game. Similarly to Duval he began the 21st century seeking major championship glory although he was runner-up to Payne Stewart at the 1999 U.S. Open.

What Duval and Leonard, Love and Mickelson, have most certainly proved is their ability to win and Notah Begay III, who did so twice in 1999 on the U.S. Tour, Rich Beem, and Brent Geiberger, who also both broke through, are among those capable of making progress. Begay is a former teammate of Woods at Stanford University and the first full-blooded Native American member of the U.S. Tour.

In his formative years he spent time living in a house on the Isleta Pueblo Reservation near Albuquerque, which is his birthplace. He said: "We had to boil hot water on a stove to take a bath. I don't come from a privileged background. My parents sacrificed a lot for me. They worked hard to put food on the table for the whole family." The ambidextrous Begay—he putts right- or left-handed depending on the contour of the green—completed an economics degree at Stanford where he was a three-time all-American and played on the 1994 N.C.A.A. championship team.

Woods said: "I've seen his determination since junior golf and all through college. He's an incredibly strong individual with a great golf ethic."

The emergence of Carlos Franco as probably the finest golfer to come out of Paraguay was all that stopped Begay from being Rookie of the Year on the U.S. Tour in 1999. Franco also won twice

Above: Hennie Otto, South Africa's great hope for the new millennium.

Right: Colin Montgomerie demonstrates his much admired swing with which he created a record of seven successive Volvo Order of Merit titles on the European Tour from 1993 to 1999.

who is a left-handed player, and South Africa's Ernie Els. Parnevik's 2000 victory in the Bob Hope Chrysler Classic, followed by another in the GTE Byron Nelson Classic four months later on the U.S. Tour, gave him further hope that in time he would enjoy success in the major championships just like Singh, who followed his 1998 U.S. P.G.A. Championship by winning the first major of the new millennium—the Masters Tournament at Augusta National.

Els celebrated his 30th birthday toward the end of 1999 but, with two U.S. Open wins to his credit, there is no question that he is a player from whom much more can be expected. Els had the natural talent to play rugby union, cricket, and golf as a youngster. He reached a scratch handicap at the age of 14 and decided to concentrate on golf. In 1992 he emulated his South African compatriot Gary Player by completing the hattrick of South African Open, P.G.A., and Masters titles and in 1994 equalled the European Tour record of 12 birdies in one round with a 61 on the way to winning the Dubai Desert Classic. He began 2000 with no fewer than 27 worldwide titles.

They call Els the "Big Easy" because of his totally relaxed manner and if, by his own admission, he had a less successful year in 1999 then there can be no question that his ability to hit the golf ball the proverbial country mile with apparently little effort coupled with a superb putting touch will bring more rewards at the highest level.

South Africa has a history of producing first class golfers. The arrival of Retief Goosen, introduced to golf at the age of 11 by his estate agent father, Theo, and a winner already of more than ten titles worldwide, and more recently that of Hennie Otto, a young man from Boksburg in

but he earned $1,864,584 compared to the $1,255,314 that Begay pocketed. Franco underlined once again to the American audience that their own players could not expect to dominate their own circuit when he made a successful defense of the Compaq Classic of New Orleans in May 2000. Australia's Stuart Appleby gained his third U.S. Tour win in 1999 when Sweden's Gabriel Hjerstedt and Jesper Parnevik also triumphed in addition to Steve Elkington, another Australian, Fiji's Vijay Singh, Canada's Mike Weir,

Gauteng who first caught the eye of the professional world when he was fifth in the 1999 South African Open at Stellenbosch, has provided new impetus for the country that has produced Bobby Locke and Gary Player, Hugh Baiocchi and John Bland, David Frost and Denis Watson.

Els, however, demonstrated during the last decade of the 20th century that he was the real thing. His motivation was simple: he wanted to be the best in the world. Since he came from a privileged background—his father owned a haulage company—the money was not a factor for Els. He had decided even before as a fresh-faced 19-year-old pre-qualifier at the 1989 Open Championship he practiced alongside Jack Nicklaus that he wanted to be the best. The best soon noted that he possessed the credentials.

Nicklaus said at that time: "There has always been talk of a dominant player and I have said that someone big and strong and with a good touch around the greens will come along. Ernie can be that one. I like the fact that he's already so mature." Player noted: "To win money, you can be a nice player. But to be that champion who finally comes along, the one people have been waiting for, you have to be like a hungry lion in a cage."

The arrival of Woods, of course, reduced the prospect of Els being that man but the internationalization of golf has seen more golfers, like Els, striving to succeed on the world stage. He is one of a number of players for whom the challenge is to finish number one on both the European and Americans Tours and he has shown that commitment by being a member of both Tours. Such a double success being completed in the same year is mouth-watering.

Colin Montgomerie dominated the European Tour in the last decade of the 20th century by finishing number one in the Volvo Order of Merit a record seven successive times from 1993 to 1999. In that time he took to 22 his number of European Tour wins and to 27 his worldwide titles. All that was missing was a major championship although he was beaten in a play-off for the 1994 U.S. Open title by Els and in a play-off for the 1995 U.S. P.G.A. Championship by Elkington in addition to finishing runner-up in the 1997 U.S. Open.

Even so the achievements of Montgomerie must be viewed from any angle as nothing short of prodigious. The game of golf in Europe has never been dominated by one man in such a way and it can be compared to the way in which the great Swedish tennis player Bjorn Borg was almost invincible for a time at Wimbledon. Montgomerie has continued to move his game to a new and higher plane with a swing that is admired by all for its supreme consistency and he continued his winning form by capturing the Norotel Perrier Open de France in May, 2000.

Mongomerie says: "I have always believed in meritocracy and have felt that I could achieve what I want if I put in sufficient effort and commitment. In recent years, a new challenge has come from a younger generation. I relish all new challenges, and while I continue to improve each year as I have strived to do over the last seven years then I know I can be competitive. As for the future, everyone wants to go out at the top and that is my aim."

Montgomerie was well aware as the new millennium began that he would face the challenge not only of his contemporaries such as Bernhard Langer and José Maria Olazábal, but also of those seeking to aspire to the very top of the class. They included Paul Lawrie, who had

Left: England's Lee Westwood came into the new millennium with 17 worldwide wins to his credit, including nine on the European Tour, and soon made it ten in Europe by winning the Deutsche Bank–SAP Open TPC of Europe by overhauling Tiger Woods with a last round of 64 at Gut Kaden, Hamburg.

Above: Thomas Bjorn of Denmark at the Heineken Golf Classic at the Vines Resort, Perth, in January 2000.

won the Open Championship in 1999, Lee Westwood, an Englishman with the credentials to follow in the footsteps of his compatriot Nick Faldo, and a young man from Northern Ireland who would make a name for himself before the 21st century was two months old.

Darren Clarke took on the world at La Costa in California in the first World Golf Championship of the year 2000 and overcame Duval in the semi-finals then Woods in the final

to win the $1,000,000 first prize at the Anderson Consulting Match Play. It was a performance that smacked of class and character as Clarke set pulses racing by taking his game to a new level and issuing a challenge to Woods's threatened domination of the sport.

In fact Clarke had long been recognized as a player with all the attributes to star on the world stage. Born in Dungannon, in Northern Ireland, in August, 1968, he enjoyed an outstanding amateur career, winning both the Irish and Spanish titles among others, before arriving on the European Tour in 1991. His victory in the Alfred Dunhill Open in 1993 threatened to light the blue touch-paper but he was compelled to wait another three years before he won again. By 1998 he had run Montgomerie close in the Volvo Order of Merit, finishing second after winning the presti-gious Volvo Masters title, but six European Tour victories were by his own admission less than satisfactory by the time he entered the year 2000.

All that was to change on the Californian coast when after moving past Paul Azinger, Thomas Bjorn, Mark O'Meara and Hal Sutton he comfortably beat David Duval then overcame Tiger Woods four and three in the final of the W.G.C.—Andersen Consulting Match Play. The American Jeff Maggert had won this title in 1999 when first it had been played, launching the World Golf Championship series, and Woods had won each of the next two World Golf Championships. There is no question that Woods was favorite to win the first main event of the 21st century but the manner in which he accepted defeat unquestionably provided further evidence of his increasing maturity. He not only warmly congratulated him but later left a

message that read: "Congrats again. Be proud." Clarke, however, had proved that Woods could be beaten and in so doing he fanned the fires of ambition burning in the hearts of many of his compatriots.

Lee Westwood, some five years younger than Clarke, regarded this achievement by his friend as a spur to himself as he pressed to continue an outstanding career that in a short time had already seen him win no fewer than 17 titles worldwide. Westwood, like so many leading golfers, was a talented sportsman at school, excelling in cricket, football, and rugby, but at the age of 13 he took up the game of golf with a half set of clubs bought for him by his grandparents. His father, John, a math teacher, took up the game at the same time to give his son encouragement and Westwood progressed through the amateur ranks before coming through the European Tour Qualifying School in 1993.

Far Right: Sergio Garcia, like
Tiger Woods, showed an
early aptitude for the game
and was the first amateur
to win the Spanish P.G.A.
title.

Westwood, probably more than any other player, threatened Montgomerie's domination in Europe as he finished third in the Volvo Order of Merit in 1997 and again in 1998, when he won four times in Europe in addition to collecting the Freeport McDermott Classic on the U.S. Tour and the

Sumitomo Visa Taiheyo Masters, with a successful defence, and Dunlop Phoenix in Japan. He followed this up by coming second in 1999.

Paul Lawrie, who had been a professional since 1986, had proved with his win in the 1999 Open Championship that there were new British

champions to follow in the footsteps of Nick Faldo, Sandy Lyle, and Ian Woosnam, although it was a young Spaniard whom many observers believed would take the challenge to Woods as the 21st century unfolded. Sergio Garcia, like Woods a child prodigy, was regarded, even by Woods himself, as a true champion in the making. "I just love watching him play," said Woods. "You can see the fire in his eyes, the emotion. He's like me in that respect—a born competitor." There is much one can compare between Garcia and Woods. At the age of two, although not a televi-

Right: Paul Lawrie enjoys his
moment of victory at the 1999
Open Championship at Carnoustie.

sion "star" like Woods, Garcia would swing a duster as if it were a golf club. Victor Garcia, his father, was the professional at the Club de Mediterraneo situated in the town of Castellon. By the age of 12 the young Garcia was recognized to be the best golfer at the club where his mother, Consuelo, managed the professionals' shop. Sergio Garcia had a handicap of scratch at the age of 13. His progress was being monitored at home and abroad, and in 1998 as an amateur he played in no fewer than 18 professional tournaments missing only one halfway cut. Furthermore he became the first amateur to win the Spanish P.G.A. title.

So comparisons with Woods were inevitable and when Garcia finished runner-up to the world number one in the 1999 U.S. P.G.A. Championship it was clearly apparent that he possessed all the attributes to compete at the highest level. They called him "El Niño"—The Boy—but he soon requested that this nickname be struck from the record books. He displayed his enthusiasm, and skill, as a first time team member for Europe in the Ryder Cup in 1999, forming a more than impressive partnership with Jesper Parnevik that helped put the United States on the rack before their final day recovery, and either side of this match he captured his first two European Tour titles—winning the Murphy's Irish Open and the Linde German Masters.

In 1999 two Spanish compatriots also enjoyed fruitful seasons. Miguel Angel Jiménez, at the age of 35, finished fourth for the second successive season in the Volvo Order of Merit when he won twice and lost only in a play off to Tiger Woods for the W.G.C.—American Express Championship at Valderrama on the Costa del Sol. Elsewhere José Maria Olazábal had won the Masters Tournament for a second time at Augusta National.

The victory by Olazábal delighted the world of golf for it confirmed his return to full health after being sidelined from the game for the best part of two years. Olazábal had been forced to withdraw from the 1995 Ryder Cup match, suffering from an illness that was eventually diagnosed as rheumatoid polyarthritis in three joints of his right foot and two in his left. There were times during those two years when, in such severe pain, he feared that he might lose the ability to walk again let alone play golf. But his bravery and persistence paid off, to everyone's immense delight.

Olazábal increased his number of worldwide victories to 26 with victory in the Benson and Hedges International Open in May, 2000 and, like Garcia he will continue to challenge for international fame and glory. The winning of the major championships—the Masters, the U.S. Open, the Open Championship, and the U.S. P.G.A. Championship—remains the ultimate goal, although the World Golf Championships will unquestionably grow in stature with history.

What the leading players win in prize money remains important, albeit that they now earn colossal sums from endorsements, but it is no longer possible to compare in financial terms what they achieve today with what the likes of Palmer and Nicklaus, Faldo and Watson, earned in the past.

Gary Player, still winning as a Senior golfer at the age of 64, pointed out: "I would not knock the generation of young players. There is some wonderful talent around. I had a practice round with Sergio Garcia—man, he was breathtaking. There is a teenage South African named Christo Greyling who is the most exciting player of his age that I have ever seen." Then Player added: "Golf will be a great game, however much money you throw at it, but consider this: David Duval won $900,000 for winning the U.S. Players Championship in 1999—in four days he won more than Ben Hogan and Sam Snead in their whole careers."

This, then, is the world of golf into which new players are emerging every year. Even so it still requires patience. Michael Campbell, of New Zealand, was within a finger touch of glory when he almost won the Open Championship in 1995. Then the magic deserted him. Campbell, however, possessed the resilience to recover and, after winning for the first time on the European

Right: Michael Campbell of New Zealand at the Johnnie Walker Classic at the Ta Shee Resort, Taiwan, in November 1999. Campbell's victory gave him a fabulous start to the 2000 European Tour International Schedule.

Tour by capturing the Johnnie Walker Classic late in 1999, he launched the new millennium as strongly as any golfer, including the mighty Tiger Woods, by winning an amazing three times within a matter of weeks. Meanwhile the Australians were delighted to unearth new talent in Brad Lamb, Brett Rumford, and Aaron Baddeley and Adam Scott.

Baddeley earned the biggest headlines when in November, 1999, he won, as an 18-year-old amateur, the Australian Open in which the likes of Nick Faldo, Colin Montgomerie, and Greg Norman were

all participants. His father, Ron, briefly a mechanic in Mario Andretti's Indy Car team in the United States where Aaron was born, and his mother, Jo-Ann, were obviously delighted although their son, unable to take the money because he had not turned professional, kept his feet on the ground. He celebrated his success by taking a few school chums to a Bondi beach pub close to Sydney and treated them to souvlaki and coke.

That, of course, is how it all begins in the world of sport. At school Aaron wanted to play cricket for Australia but, like so many others

Left: Australia's Aaron Baddeley at the New Zealand Open at Paraparamu Beach, Wellington, in January 2000.

before him, he became engrossed by the game of golf after being invited to swing a club by one of his grandparents. He reached a scratch handicap at the age of 15, he plastered his bedroom with pictures of the great golfers, and, after winning his Club Championship at the age of 14 in 1995, he received a letter from none other than Jack Nicklaus, who had read Aaron was a promising youngster and wished him well.

Ian Baker-Finch, the Australian who won the Open Championship in 1991, said: "He has all the ingredients to be an Australian Tiger Woods. I've never seen an 18-year-old who is so level-headed and well-balanced. When I was 18 I'd just finished my apprenticeship as a professional and I wasn't a patch on this kid—that's for sure!"

Meanwhile, in America, heads were being turned by two 22-year-old British golfers, Paul Casey and Luke Donald. There are few tougher schools in sport than the American universities and, as 1999 unfolded, so the talk was of Casey, studying at Arizona State, and Donald, who was at Northwestern, near Chicago, becoming part of

Right: Tiger Woods at the 1999
American Express World Golf
Championship held at Valderama,
Spain.

the new era of professional golf. They were ranked one and two on the U.S. college circuit and, like Baddeley, they appeared in no hurry to turn professional, although clearly it was only a matter of time. Instead they were prepared to go through their own apprenticeship, enjoying experiences such as being part of the winning Great Britain and Ireland Walker Cup team in 1999, and, like the American Matt Kuchar, the 1997 U.S. Amateur Champion, were gaining in experience all the time. In 1999 Donald was named the college player of the year in the United States where he broke several records, many of which had been set by Tiger Woods, and at Hazeltine he became the first European to win the N.C.A.A. Championship.

There were others, too, like Justin Rose, who turned professional after finishing fourth in the Open Championship when still only 17 years old, Nick Dougherty, and Philip Rowe. Rose, who first swung a club (albeit a plastic version) in his back garden at the age of 11, was born in South Africa but he moved to England at the age of five when he started to play seriously. By the age of 11 Rose had broken 70 and, following his supreme performance in the Open Championship at Royal Birkdale, he plunged into the professional pool where he initially struggled before winning his card for the European Tour at the 1999 Qualifying School.

Others preferred to stay amateur to hone their game for the move to the professional stage. Dougherty, who came under the tutelage of Nick Faldo, preferred not to take up offers from American colleges although he did win the Polo Classic, a leading American junior tournament, while Rowe gained one of the "hottest tickets in golf" when he was awarded a Tiger

Woods scholarship to Stanford University in the year 2000. Rowe had won all three of his matches in the 1999 Walker Cup and in so doing defeated the American Matt Kuchar each time.

In America, Kuchar was highly regarded, along with others such as David Gossett and Bryce Molder, as an amateur golfer likely to progress to challenge for the leading honors on offer in the game. Winning the 1997 U.S. Amateur swept Kuchar, from the suburb of Lake Mary in Orlando, Florida, into the spotlight and he finished 21st in the 1998 U.S. Masters and 14th in the U.S. Open two months later. Even so he elected to complete his degree at Georgia Tech which he was due to leave in June, 2000.

At the time Gossett, from Germantown, Tennessee, was in his second year of a degree at the University of Texas from where he had gone out to win the 99th U.S. Amateur in 1999 by beating the Korean Amateur Champion Sung Yoon Kim by nine and eight in the 36 hole final. His reward for that achievement was to be able to tee-up as an amateur in the 2000 Masters Tournament, U.S. Open, and Open Championship at Augusta National, Pebble Beach, and St. Andrews respectively. In other words Gossett had earned the right to live the dream of all aspiring golfers—to tread in the shoes of Old Tom Morris and Harry Vardon, Bobby Jones and Gene Sarazen, Ben Hogan and Gary Player, Arnold Palmer and Jack Nicklaus, Severiano Ballesteros and Nick Faldo, and to move on to challenge Tiger Woods as a new millennium in the great game of golf began to unfold.

Left: The sun sets over the 17th green at Augusta National Golf Club, scene of so many great golfing moments.

INDEX